FASHION ON THE BEAT

FASHION ON THE BEAT

THE MELODIES AND RHYTHMS IN FASHION JOURNALISM

GIULIA BALDINI

NEW DEGREE PRESS

FASHION ON THE BEAT

The Melodies and Rhythms in Fashion Journalism

ISBN   978-1-64137-931-1 *Paperback*

978-1-64137-726-3 *Kindle Ebook*

978-1-64137-727-0 *Ebook*

I dedicate this book to those people who love life, who are willing to love life, who have pledged to a lovely life

CONTENTS

―――

INTRODUCTION

———

Dear Readers,

Class of 2020 has graduated and here we are with our diplomas in the air. Congratulations!

Although many of us are happy and relieved, some of us graduates feel a bit somber and unsure of their future. Maybe "some of these graduates" is just a nice way to say "I, Giulia, am feeling a bit somber and unsure of my future," but if there's someone else out there who's feeling down and is wondering why and how these cloudy feelings are upon them...

I'm telling you, welcome to the club: Congratulations!

I had imagined that I would have written a different kind of introduction for this book, something light and positive. You know, something that you can read and feel relieved. I pivoted onto another path: I wanted to write you something extremely real, including how I feel about the situations that have shaken us all up: COVID 19, Black Lives Matter, and their consequences. And sure, fashion, journalism, and all that jazz.

After four years of studies in journalism, if there's something that my professors and mentors have instilled and inspired in me, it's to pursue fairness in reporting facts, matters, and stories. In my short time in the fashion industry, I've learned that changes are nothing less than opportunities to learn from and navigate. With the challenging times we're all experiencing, I've learned to take the present moments as they are and accept the changes that our most popular industries are performing.

We must recognize a crisis, a big one, in both journalism and fashion. A crisis that has to do with money, racism, sexism, and many other fields full of inequities. Everything we were trained for and looking forward to embarking into is swirling around new dynamics and circumstances. We need to find solutions and be realistic. We need to find shifts in uncomfortable spaces. In this book I want to be real. I don't want to share sad stories because my life has been everything but sad. However, I don't want to tell you only the glamour and the amazing opportunities that have come my way. This book is an open letter to the fashion industry, the journalism industry, and all those industries that require an intersectional and creative mindset.

The sudden absence of a commencement doesn't make me feel sad per se, although I would have loved a traditional celebration. Graduating from college would've been the one and only academic celebration to enjoy with the company of my mom and dad. Even though my dad has earned a university degree, I would've been the first person in my family to graduate in another country from an institution of higher education. I was supposed to spend these days and commencement day with my best friends from home and my dearest American ones.

I imagined myself with my big afro, nails done, makeup, a cute dress, and boom, throwing the cap up in the air, the ultimate gesture that any student, especially any international student, dreams of doing after spending long semesters at an American college. By May I was supposed to have finished a whole manuscript that took a lot of time and courage to pour out. But here I am, believing in my potential and crafting my own voice amid the chaos. Plans have changed, but the content of this book hasn't that much. It just got deeper and deeper until the very last day of submitting the manuscript to my editors. God bless them!

My concerns and preoccupations are related to employment and adulthood. Mondays go by and I don't go to school anymore. What will my routine look like, for real this time? I can't have my dream job yet. And after that? How do I say no to certain jobs and yes to others? I don't know how to allow myself to be bored, I can't spend time doing nothing. I'm embarking on the bureaucratic processes that thousands of immigrants every day have to deal with. I wish I could do all this with someone close to me or open to listen to me. However, I am always afraid of boring people. We're all facing an extreme situation, so why would my problems be interesting or relevant?

I've always longed for this moment: adulthood. When I was in middle school, I couldn't wait to be a writer in New York, probably in the Upper East Side. Just like Carrie Bradshaw in Sex and the City. In high school, I wanted to be a screenwriter based between New York and Los Angeles. Just like a female version of Truman Capote. In college, I wanted to focus just on New York and be a journalist, a fashionista, a fashion journalist, an entrepreneur, and an entrepreneurial fashion journalist. It all escalated so quickly to be honest, and little did I know that time would fly.

So here I am thinking about how I should invest my time during these uncertain circumstances. No matter how many plans and tactics I have, I still must wait and depend on major authorities and forces. What will happen to my dreams? Will there be anyone I will be able to share those dreams of mine with, or should I keep my voice down? Are my dreams relevant? Do I even deserve to be happy in such a difficult world?

I've just graduated from college, and we all know that college brings a lot of memories, pain, and satisfactions. As an international student, I have lived here in the U.S. for four years, and my personal experience with academia, friendships, boys, and self-love has been a unique roller coaster of emotions and reflections. Even though we all have different backgrounds, I believe that my story is as unique as many others. But here I am feeling that all my emotional and academic work isn't going to pay off, including the all-nighters and tears I've shed during these four years. What will make me stand out? Will I ever have friends for life that will stick with me no matter what? Will my romantic feelings go away forever since I don't believe in love anymore like before? Why am I so numb right now, but at the same time full of life? Sheesh, I get so rational, but now I smile more than ever, even though times are harder. Am I crafting my voice, right? What is even right or wrong?

I'm sure this is a temporary series of turbulent feelings that I can't avoid experiencing. Being in the middle of a devastating pandemic and unexpected economic recession hurts everyone. I keep typing on my laptop, and my ideas are bursting out more than ever, which is a good sign. It means that my brain is motivated, and my dreams are not dead at all.

Sometimes I cry because I think this is so unfair. I've always wanted to help, but it seems that I can't do much these days, besides being good to myself at my best. Watching George Floyd's death and Breonna Taylor's case, I keep thinking how these things are still happening in a country that is supposed to be founded under the idea of equality, dreamers, and freedom. Where am I? What am I doing here? Where am I standing with my own story?

I keep hearing over and over again how sweet and lovely I am, but every day I become more and more Holly Golightly, with less faith in personal affections and global justice. I've always wanted to be close to my friends, but now I can't see all of them, and I don't know how much I matter to them. Every time I receive a call or a message from them my heart is full, but I don't want to bore them with my concerns. I miss my family, but when will the time arrive when I can buy the most beautiful vacation I can afford for my mom and dad? When will I be financially free and independent? How and when can I flex, real talk?

Note: I swear to you, the core and juice of the book is coming. Keep reading. These words will make sense at the end of this introduction. Also, before someone thinks I'm that kind of pessimistic person when it comes to love or faith in the world:

I am not. Those questions come and go. These are concerns that travel in my mind, and I let them be legitimate, but certainly not the focus of my goals and principles I believe in. Sometimes I'm just worried because all I can think is: "I'm twenty-three and I still haven't landed on that job, gig, opportunity, etc." But since I've learned to shut down these voices, I've adopted this strategy: welcome these thoughts, let them swirl around in my head, box them, and trash them. Let's keep rolling.

My attention is targeted only to a certain type of content when I'm surfing on the internet, looking for articles to read, liking pictures on Instagram, funny tweets on Twitter, and soothing images on Pinterest and Tumblr. Sometimes I come across romantic couples, families all together, beautiful houses, traveling spots I've always longed to go to, nails and hairstyles on point, and healthy, scrumptious foods that I can't afford at the moment . . . and my heart sinks a bit, because I feel happy, grateful, and blessed for my situation, despite it all, but . . . what now? Why can't I have these things too? Am I bad? Nah, not at all. Will my graduation matter and help me get nice things in life? What are the nice things in life? What's nice for me? It's not a constant thought, but it's the type of thought that when you get it, it lasts some long minutes in your head. But then it goes away. Because at the end of the day, you know you're that golden star. At least, I know. I know how grateful I am, but it's okay to lose sight and wonder how I'm doing. Once I came to accept this thing, I came across my own balance: I know and love myself just the way I am.

Now, you might think you're holding the wrong book in your hands. I can see you thinking: "Why is she pouring out this stream of consciousness? Wasn't this book supposed to be about fashion and journalism? Where are the clothes, the interviews, and the crazy college stories?"

To dream and keep my heart at a reasonable beat I listen to Jhené Aiko, Drake, slow Beyoncé, and Rihanna jams, with a splash of Bad Bunny's "Solo De Mi" and a curated bossa nova playlist. Right now, I am listening to Drake's "Signs."[1]

You wanna drink like Bajan and dance like Trini

Yeah

You want a supermodel pose like mi real friend Winnie

Yeah

I've always liked these lyrics for various reasons. One of these is the sense of freedom they give me and the memories and dreams I've attached to them. "Signs" is one of the few songs I've secretly treasured in my heart in college.

But now the melodies and the beats will change with a new fashion in vogue! Yes, fashion will produce new music to our ears, and journalism will catch and narrate its beats. A new fashion era will be on its beat.

---

1   Drake, "Signs."

Welcome to Fashion on the Beat, written by Giulia, the curly flower. Some of these words are taken from my blog, some were exclusively and largely written just for this book. Thank you in advance for your taking time to read this mumbo jumbo of mine. But you know what they say about the crazy ones. They change the world.

I'll probably just spark a smile in you, and for me that'll be life changing!

Beijos,

the curly flower

CHAPTER 1

PAST, PRESENT, FUTURE, AND WHERE I STAND AS A FASHION WRITER

——

An apple
because it's said
to be sweet,
to taste good

Lots of sayings around.

Rice and beans
to feed the kids,
granny, and Uncle Lou

There are others
Not just you.

Chocolate and vanilla
to make a cake

It's for fun's sake.

Two water bottles
To keep the flower's sap
flowing

Push that cart on
life must go on.

Grocery's list
- *items for a rich life*

I have always been fascinated by something about the summer, especially the Italian summer. Colors and citrusy scents come to mind, but what really has an impact on me is the warmth, the sounds of the waves at the seaside, and the bicycle rides in the countryside.

I was born and raised in Florence, by an Italian dad and a Brazilian mom. I grew up speaking two languages at home, Italian and Portuguese. Until I was ten years old, I traveled around Europe and back and forth from Italy to Brazil every two years. Through these trips I've been collecting unforgettable memories and affections worth a lifetime.

Most of the time I am in awe of the work and tasks that the human brain can do. Think about it: the brain is connected with literally every single organ that we have and is the source where our dreams, thoughts, and affections reside. Sure, the heart is fundamental, and it needs to beat to maintain our existence. But what makes a human being that exceptional creature full of aspirations and emotions is the brain. For this reason, I've always been fascinated by the brain's job. One thing that most intrigues me about the human psyche is memory, or the ability to remember episodes of our lives.

THE LAST FASHIONABLE PERSON: HOW I GOT INTO FASHION

April 2014. High school was quite tiring back then. I had difficult classmates and severe professors demanding a high quantity of homework. Written and oral tests were about to come up. A typical anxious and diligent student like me was feeling pretty overwhelmed. I remember being extremely stressed over some homework I was trying to finish. I don't recall what the exact subject was, but I was probably dealing with something really complicated like Latin or math. Through the window in my bedroom, I could see the clear and vibrant sky, tempting me to leave every chore and go outside. That sky was so beautiful, and I couldn't stay anymore over the books. The temptation won.

I called my friend Isa and asked her if I could go to her house. Isa was the kind of girl who was always there for people when they needed her and would always welcome her friends at her place. Back then I admired her lifestyle so much. She was the kind of girl every boy wanted to date, every girl wanted to be friends with, every parent wished they had because of her kindness and strength. Isa probably wasn't the A student that many teachers wished she were, but she was and still is one of the smartest people I know in my life. She learns and fails with grace and perseverance, with a balance that not many people can embrace. I never had the chance to be free-spirited like her during my high school years. However, despite the huge amount of fun I had with her, when I was around her, I felt I was still in a sort of "school": the school of life.

Isa gave me so many life lessons, talking about boys, friendships, family. Isa was a trendy friend, but also a cool teacher in her own way. That sunny day with that crispy blue Tuscan sky I reached Isa at her place and together we went to her friend's house, a big, marvelous mansion that overlooked all of Florence. Isa, her friend, and another boy who joined us later had decided to meet up for a photoshoot. At the time, these photoshoots had only one purpose: taking pictures for social media, specifically Facebook. Nowadays we could all smile, or even laugh at these practices, but imagine a bunch of teenagers in the 2010s looking for establishing themselves online with their creative ventures and artistic skills. We only had Tumblr, Facebook, and Ask.fm. Some of us had MySpace or Instagram, but at the time the big deal was Facebook. At least in Florence among my friends' group.

"Why are you guys taking pictures?"

"It's for our Facebook profile picture."

I looked at them skeptically. Why would someone waste their time taking professional pictures for a social media photo profile? What's the fun? My mind was so rigid back then because I was terrified of exposing myself on the World Wide Web.

The first time I had a social media profile was the day I set up a Facebook account. I remember I was scared to do so because my dad had terrified me with stories of young people getting onto social media. As a dad he didn't want me to get in the loop of these practices. He believed that social media platforms were just like video games. He would say "Your brain will be fried," "You won't study on books anymore," "You won't read or learn," and the most fearful warning: "You're gonna waste time."

During my teens, I never wanted to go against my father or mother because I didn't want to become the cliché daughter with common problems weighing on her adolescence. For this reason, my self-defense mechanism was being a "good girl," if there's even a real definition for this concept. We all make mistakes, right? Even the most innocent human beings. Luckily, I genuinely liked to study, read, and learn new subjects in school, but many other aspects of my life didn't bloom during this period. I never followed the crowd, never talked about politics in front of my family, and never explored any other interests except theatre and swimming. I was lucky and blessed to be comfortable in my own spaces, but with hindsight I can say that I wasn't as flexible and bubbly as I am now. It took me a whole college experience overseas to finally find my inner child and bring her back to the surface again, with no shame or regret.

I made my Facebook profile because it was required for school. I remember it was a science project, the year was 2012, and I had to get on the class group chat for exchanging materials and videos for the course. My friend Susanna helped me do that. I recall that day as clear as the sun, specifically the moment I had clicked on my fresh Facebook profile. Listen, I had lied to my dad once. In second grade he told me to not eat from other children's snacks during recess, but a classmate offered me a single Wacko's chip and I was too tempted to say no.

Fast forward eight years, this white lie can go on too. It has to. At the end of the day, I was doing this for school. Susanna was so helpful, and that day meant a lot to me. The gesture was little, but it was the first time I had said a firm "no" to my parents, especially to my dad, without feeling any regret. When my dad found out I had Facebook, after two or three weeks I believe, he didn't freak out as much as I thought he would. He was disappointed, he scoffed, but he didn't give me any particular lecture or stare. That day I felt free and I started gaining a bit more confidence in my own decisions.

Once I had Facebook, of course, I expanded my academic use to a personal one. Thanks to Facebook, I was connected with the world, my friends, and some family in Brazil, without having to go to a payphone or calling them from my house. I still wasn't familiar with WhatsApp back in 2012. Two years went by, and here I am with Isa and her friends to get a new profile picture for Facebook. The girls were looking for locations, while smiling, giggling, and just having fun. The boy was taking pictures, and he seemed to have fun too. He was an amateur photographer. I was just standing out of the scene holding Isa's friend's dog. I was feeling both left out and awkward watching them. I had a complex that sometimes still comes out today, but in a much softer way. I wasn't feeling cute enough to be in a picture nor did I want to put myself out there on the internet. I knew social media wasn't bad, but I still had those thoughts my dad had put in my brain. I could see girls on this app called Instagram with big hair like me, and I wanted to take pictures like that, but neither my friends nor family were very much into this or pushed me to do it. So, I lost faith and let it go. I wasn't cute enough in real life, just a geek. Might as well continue this way. "Let's keep writing, stay in school, no modeling or acting," I'd say. I could never be in front of a camera, never. I wasn't my four-year-old self, the Giulia who wanted to be a ballerina at Teatro Verdi. I was having these kinds of thoughts when Isa's friend approached me:

"Do you want to take a picture, too?"

"No, I look horrible. I'm not dressed well."

"Don't say that. Give it a shot, come on."

One minute later I was sitting on the grass, next to a tree trunk, and trying to smile at the camera lens. A couple of weeks later that photo would become my new Facebook profile picture. When I went back home that afternoon, I thought how fun it was actually taking outdoor pictures while hanging out with friends. I enjoyed making those moments memorable with the mere presence of a camera.

In June 2014, after hanging out with Isa, I saw a little potential in me. I didn't have the guts to flaunt it or to showcase it, but for whatever reason I found a new comfort zone in being in front of a camera when I was hanging out with my friends. I liked taking pictures as well as modeling. Having a good break between my long hours of studying was fun. I could embrace as many alter egos as possible. The photoshoot was like acting, but without a script, so a little bit looser. But I could do this only in front of my few female friends. I was discovering modeling, but I never got scouted, instructed on the industry, or even introduced to what a model is. All I knew was that these pictures would eventually end up on my Facebook timeline, just like a LinkedIn profile picture, to share with my few hundreds of friends. Nothing less, nothing more. I was literally having fun.

In 2014, I took my first train trip alone to Rome. I was visiting my Roman friends Chiara and Flavia. I met Chiara and Flavia in Porto Santo Stefano, a small town in the South of Tuscany, where my family and I would spend our summer vacations. Chiara, Flavia, and their little brother Andrea clicked right away with me since I was ten years old. Without sugar coating, I think that I spent some of my most marvelous days with them, swimming at the beach (at Siluripedio), sailing from coast to coast (in the promontory of Argentario), and eating ice creams (at Gelateria Giulia), pizzas (so many pizzas), and anything scrumptious you could think of both in their kitchen and at my house.

That year I decided to go alone to Rome and visit them for a weekend. We were playing around their living room, jumping from one activity to another: reading a book, watching a movie, sunbathing on the balcony, eating snacks, and doing makeup and hairstyles. It was a mix of activities with them. I could never get bored. Whenever I would hang out with them, even if I were the older one, I felt like I was back when I was four years old, hyperactive and smiley 24/7, but with much more awareness of my actions, of course. With Chiara and Flavia, I was always my true self. We would set up comedy sketches at the beach. We would even write our own stories, play the characters, and present little shows, dances, and open-mic nights in front of our families. I'm smiling while typing these words and recollecting these memories. But back to the story. As an Italian, I have this weird habit of mine to open long parenthesis and stream of consciousness. Is that an Italian thing, an Aquarius thing, or just a Giulia thing? Anyway, back to that day in the neighborhood of Balduina, Rome.

Between one thing and another, we ended up surfing the internet. We were probably just looking up Zac Efron or some trendy boy from an American TV show or music band like Big Time Rush. Those were the years, don't judge. We were in their parents' studio and I remember Chiara bringing up a camera out of the blue. "This is my mom's camera, there's still battery." We put some music on and we started dancing to our favorite songs: Taylor Swift, Miley Cyrus, and any song from any Disney Channel original, with some will.i.am, Bruno Mars, and Pharrell Williams ("Happy," anyone?). Then I decided to dress up and put some makeup on (just mascara, eye pencil, and foundation because I had just learned how to apply makeup, and I wanted to show them my new skill).

After that, while Flavia and I were dancing, Chiara started taking candids of us, jumping around the room, with and without flash. I started posing and pretending to be a fashion model, while I was having the goofiest time with Flavia, with our tongues out and funny faces, following the beats of the music playing on the computer. That one was one of my favorite afternoons spent in the Eternal City. I would keep this tradition with them until the next year, in 2015, just before spending my first month at the ESL program in Riverdale at the College of Mount Saint Vincent, where I would meet another photographer and creative person: Coco.

February 2015. In Italy, we celebrate our sweet eighteen, instead of the American sweet sixteen, or the Latino quinceañera. For my birthday that year, I wanted to do a photoshoot, or at least recreate something fun like I did with Isa and her friend. I got all dressed up for the occasion, with a white pearl business shirt, an H&M red and black Scottish skirt, underneath which I was wearing thick black tights with a pair of blue and red French chunky high heels. I did the makeup by myself and put a simple outfit together. It was both pretty formal and elegant. My friends and I took a series of photos, not only of me. Every one of us got the chance to get a shot while wandering in the cold and windy Florence city center. I was born on the day of love, Valentine's Day. Florence is super cold during February. But with much love and sass, my friends and I were taking the city by storm.

After that occasion I went to Rome, and even though I did a second photoshoot with Chiara and Flavia at their house, I decided not to be in any more photos from that moment on. Even though I knew I looked good, I was dealing with too many worries inside my head: college admissions, moving to another country, and my self-esteem, which was decreasing more and more. This time was also after "the green lipstick episode," which you will learn about in the next chapters. Plus, I had cut my hair very short, changed the color, and I was still not very confident in showing it off, especially in front of a camera.

My spirit lifted again the summer of 2015, when I met Coco, one of my dearest Italian friends who spent a year in New York City. Coco and I met in the ESL program at the College of Mount Saint Vincent. When I met Coco, my confidence was zero, if not less. I was extremely skinny, underweight, and in search of my own representation, someone to look up to, without being on the books or in an academic setting. One day, Coco decided to cheer me up by inviting me to her place, eating some Italian food, and hanging out in the city. At the time, Coco was an amateur photographer, and I was her model whenever she needed a person. She taught me the basics of photography, modeling, and blogging. Two Italians in New York, sharing the American dream, with its struggles and downsides. Just like with Isa, Coco was a teacher in her own way from the school of life, giving me lessons on boys, friendships, and art. With Coco the connection was deeper because for some time we shared a goal. Studying and living in the U.S. was something that nobody back home could get on board with me. Even two years later, when Coco left the U.S. and decided to pursue her studies in Italy, I still kept a strong connection with her because she instantly understood me, and she knew what situations I was dealing with. Again, I had fun with Coco as I learned tons through her. And during this day in New York with Coco I was thinking about how to turn that fun into something constructive and real. Hence, I started to think about the world of fashion, seriously this time.

When I moved to go to college in New York, my personality abruptly changed. While I thought it was going to be the opposite of a comfort zone, I found a lot of welcoming people at first who engaged with me and were curious about my background. For the first time, somebody was actually interested in hearing my stories or found my story similar to theirs. In Italy people weren't very invested in knowing what my half Brazilian part meant to me. I was more Italian than

Brazilian for them. On the other hand, I was too Italian for my Brazilian family, and that bothered me for a long time. I simply couldn't understand why I couldn't be equally Italian and Brazilian.

People were always telling me how much my hair was so different and trendy, unique and great in the U.S. For this reason, I gradually changed the perception of myself and started being more confident in my look. See, when I was in middle school, I hated my hair: extremely curly and so different from the other girls'. Back in high school, I got tired of straightening it just to look like most of the people around me. I decided to cut it and gradually started embracing my hair the way it has always been–curly, puffy, and voluptuous.

Although people's comments were the thing that pushed me into fashion, my journey into fashion occurred in a moment of my life where I needed to find self-love, while finding out my likes, dislikes, and goals. It's still an ongoing journey, but the milestones I was able to conquer through the colors, the shades, and the beats that this industry presented me with were immense.

When I started studying at Hofstra, the courses I was enrolled in weren't as interesting as I had envisioned. In fact, before coming to New York in 2016, I was so sure that to attend college with an academic schedule would satisfy all my academic preferences: little natural science, no math, a lot of English, and some acting. What more could I ask? That was the dream. Even though the courses were interesting, by the time I had been at Hofstra for three full semesters I found myself bored and annoyed by the things I was learning in the classrooms.

I wasn't enjoying screenwriting, the literature classes, and the endless readings I had to complete for my elective courses anymore. In the meantime, fashion articles and entertainment issues, like movies, TV shows, and music became the only things I enjoyed reading. They were conversational and educative, fun to read and easy to engage. They could enhance my reading and writing skills, while also getting me informed on a lot of stuff that my peers were talking about, but I didn't know—American pop culture.

Especially during the first year, college students do a lot of ice breakers. As an international student, I was expected to engage in these activities with not only my American classmates, but also (if not primarily) with the other international kids. Most of the international students I've come across these years have been Asians, followed by Africans, Latinos, and Europeans. My interaction with Italians and Italian culture dropped the moment I started my classes at Hofstra. For four years, I've met only three Italian people on the whole campus but never got the chance to hang out with them due to our different schedules. Given the circumstances, the only language I was expected to practice was solely and exclusively English. When I was asked questions like "What is your favorite movie?" or "Who's your favorite actress?" I would give still answers, with references that few people knew about. "My favorite movie is Breakfast at Tiffany's with Audrey Hepburn."

Kids would look at me and think that I was so old school. I didn't have a problem with that, I wouldn't go against my choices. But the more these questions came up regarding my music preferences, favorite TV shows (Gossip Girl aficionado here in the building!), and movies (from Some Like It Hot with Marilyn Monroe to Alfred Hitchcock's The Rope), I started feeling a bit out of place, and the only thing I could do was to either keep my preferences just the way they were or peek at other stuff I could like too. I chose the second option. It wasn't an instant choice.

Growing up in Florence wasn't easy as a creative person. I had clogged my creative vein because I simply wanted to avoid my parents' opinions on my preferences and my choices. I'll tell you a story that will make you understand what I mean by saying this.

One day I was listening to Rihanna's "Man Down" in the living room. I was doing a homemade facial with sugar, honey, and hot-boiled water. While I was pampering myself with the honey and sugar on my damp face, my father came into the living room and commented on the song. Of course, he didn't like the song. He said it sounded dumb. I said I liked it. We went back and forth with this discussion, and I remember that I was so pissed off about my dad's narrow-mindedness in terms of artistic choices, directions, and interests, I simply couldn't get why he was against me listening to reggae or rap, as he was the first one in the house to say to me to be receptive and curious about other sounds. I didn't get why I had to listen to Bach's melodies all the time and not some Rihanna, Amy Winehouse (he thought Amy Winehouse was a bad example to follow. I get his point when you think about her lifestyle and the way she ended up engaging with despicable substances, but I still don't get why he would not encourage me to listen to her, who happens to be one of my favorite artists) or even Adele. And the crazy thing was that he loved Norah Jones (I love her very much too), who was basically another version of Adele and Amy Winehouse. Our beats weren't in sync for these dumb reasons. I vowed that one day soon I would get out of that home and blast whatever music I wanted to listen to and sing along with at maximum volume. But this was a call I was making for myself. I made a mental note to explore and dig into my curiosities and passions once I was able to travel and live abroad. Well, that day came and even to this day, I listen to music that my father would never approve of. This is life, kids. It's like that sometimes with people from older generations

My musical choices never coincided with my dad's. I was lucky to like some of his favorite musicians, like Frank Zappa, and genres like jazz, blues, and classical music, but he was never the kind of dad who was open to listening to other sounds or even open to having conversations about fashion or anything artistic that didn't pertain to what academia calls "classic." For this reason, a lot of the American movies I would watch were from the early 50s to the late 70s.

For this reason, I never wanted to hear his opinions on what I was listening to or watching on TV at my friends' or by myself on the internet. I would only talk to my mom whose musical taste was much more like mine. I remember listening to lots of Michael Jackson, Amy Winehouse, Whitney Houston, Aretha Franklin, Sade, and Alicia Keys with her. She didn't like rap, and to be honest she didn't know much about it either. But when I was four and five years old, she would always support my theatrical performances in front of the TV, singing and dancing with those old MTV videos (anyone remember Beyoncé's "Crazy In Love" and Black Eyed Peas' "Don't Lie?" I'm that old indeed).

This kind of spontaneous behavior was very much approved by mom, but way less by my dad, who has always hoped for me to have an academic mindset. But I wasn't like that, and now I'm sure I will never be like that. However, my parents' balance and lifestyles made me realize how much education and strict rules are important and fundamental, as much as allowing yourself to have fun and love what you're doing. Both behaviors have been imperative and important to me, even when my dad was very strict and stubborn. I'm glad I took a break from living at home and have explored another continent without any help from my family and friends from back home. It has been hard, but such a rewarding experience that I will always be grateful for. Every day I wake up thinking how blessed I have been to live and study in New York City, travel to places I could've never imagined, and learn every tiny bit of information—from school to literally anything else—by myself. These last four years opened new conversations between my parents and me. If you ask my mom now who Drake or Donald Glover or even Lil Wayne is, she knows them all! If you ask my dad what my favorite readings and journalists are, he will give you a solid answer, whether he agrees or disagrees with my point of view. I know that this is not always the case, but I think that with distance, both physically and mentally, I was able to find myself and to reconnect with my roots and family in a healthy way. It feels weird to say that I've found home in a totally different place than where I grew up. It feels crazy to say that I could feel comfortable anywhere I end up being, but that's because I've found peace in myself, my choices, perspectives, and lifestyle decisions. I will always thank my parents for allowing me the experience to study abroad. The only genre that would dominate in our house was bossa nova and Jazz. This explains a lot. Now you know why when I came here, my knowledge of rap, trap, hip-hop, and American movies was extremely narrow. Back to the Hofstra days, my first year.

During that time, I was hanging out a lot with Khin Su, my future roommate for three years in college. We clicked right away. Just like me, Khin Su didn't know much about American culture either, even though she was much more into modern TV shows and movies than I was. We had come from such different cultures—one from Italy, one from Myanmar—yet we converged into the same place of learning and discovering, as college students, but also as young cosmopolitan women.

Along with Khin Su, Joyce was my very first friend at Hofstra. She was in the same department and like me, she was into movies. She was not only the bridge between Khin Su and me, but also our personal teacher on American pop culture. In fact, she was the first person to introduce me to Frank Ocean, Donald Glover, Solange, and Tyler, The Creator. Then I met Tyrone, who was working as an RA and knew a lot of people at the International Students Affair offices and clubs. As an Afro-Latino kid, Tyrone was the first person to teach me and remind of something that I had forgotten about my upbringing: my Blackness. Being Black or non-white is a universal experience, and I knew that very well. But being African American was a different story, a story whose chapters I didn't know much about. Through our conversations, he made me realize how much I still did not know about the USA. In all those years in school I had been instructed on certain facts, but how about police brutality? How about systemic racism? How about rap, trap, reggae, soca, and even samba, things that were part of me when I was little, but that for a long time had been repressed?

For this reason, in addition to these conversations, I used my fashion magazine to get onto the news, to get a hint of what was popping, what was not, and what the trends could become. Fashion would not only allow me to dream, but also keep my eyes on the ground.

Fashion has become my home, my temple, and my shelter. I don't own a large amount of clothes, but I do have a knack for making the most creative and elegant ensembles. When I was younger, I had this image of myself in my twenties: walking in Paris, holding a cup of coffee, with all my majestic hair being shown off. I just had no idea of how I could achieve that status. I still don't, to be honest. I've never thought that I, Giulia Baldini, could be interested in fashion. If I must say, with all the transparency of a curly flower, I'm the least fashionable person ever. Well, I have to be clearer. I do have a style and some sort of natural elegance, but when it comes to trends and new hits, I might be that slow fashionista who catches them after two weeks, or even two months. However, now fashion has become my home, my temple, and my shelter.

At first, it was like being in a fantastic introspection. In fashion I could find a shelter made of comforting colors and vibrant hues that didn't need words to be captured. You just need an eye for detail to appreciate fashion and its productions. However, shortly after this realization of mine, I was feeling the urgency to find other ways to experience fashion, not only with my body. Being on a college campus in the suburbs didn't allow me to be in direct contact with the typical fashion bits, gigs, and such that could've kept me in the loop with the latest trends and events. For this reason, my solution to this temporary inconvenience was writing, reporting, and using my academic assignments to go to and attend these events, explore the city in the shoes of a brown Carrie Bradshaw. It was a matter of priorities: should I put my passion first or school? Did I invest my time and finances to pursue an education or a career? What if I stick to my main plan and incorporate however I can my other passions? So, I mixed pleasure with work, and fashion with journalism. Little did I know that becoming a fashion journalist would become my vocation and ultimately my goal.

MY STYLE

I'm gonna keep it real with you. If I follow your personal account on Instagram, you must fit under these categories, or at least one: I like your aesthetics, I learn from you, or I love you. If you happen to inspire me, keep me educated, and support me through your actions, then it's a win-win situation. That's how I build my style.

I consider style the design and the appeal you apply to your life. Style influences your education, your ways, manners, and thoughts in life. And of course, the way you dress up and present yourself to others. Being able to display a style or make one of your own is a form of freedom.

I wouldn't say my style has dramatically changed over the span of ten full years, but I can affirm a transition of likes and dislikes that have shaped my wardrobe over the years.

My very first memory of styling has a Brazilian setting. I was in fact on a bus traveling from my family's hometown, Nova Iguacu to the city of Rio de Janeiro. My mom was sitting next to me, and I remember her looking at me a bit skeptically during our commute. I had taken her purple shirt, which was oversized for my chest and waist, and paired it up with a long, over-the-knee demi-skirt and a pair of sneakers. The whole outfit was a success to me, on the border line of edginess and trendy. To my mom this look appeared weird, but somehow appealing. She said that it was okay—nothing to be worried about. A few years later, the baggy shirts, the long demi-skirts, and the bulky sneakers became a trend. Now, I'm not saying I'm a visionary, but I can say I have a sixth sense about what styles or trends will take off. I don't know how I possess this ability, but I do have it.

I've always had a thing for being edgy and acting out of the box. I think this is due to my ethnic background, especially because of my Blackness in an environment predominately white.

Summer 2015. Before spending a month in Riverdale, New York, at the College of Mount Saint Vincent, I did a brief vacation in Castiglione della Pescaia. I was at my best friend's grandma's house. I was with her and another friend we had in common. Those days were really beautiful, and I will always cherish the moments I have spent there. It was my first time going to this little but pretty well-known town, and I was just very happy to spend a couple of days with my dear friends. That vacation was not only fun, but also an eye-opening experience. I spent the first two or three days just going to the beach and hanging out with my friend's group. It was fun, the place was beautiful with its clear water, warm sunsets, and home-cooked meals. In addition to all that, on one of those evenings and for the first time in my life, I kissed a boy on the lips.

I laugh and smile at this memory because it was the most awful kiss I've ever given and received, but it was such a thrill telling the story and talking about it with my friend. The same night I tried hard liquor at the bar for the first time too. Just to give you an idea on how naive and goofy I was, I'll tell you what happened on that occasion. That night was supposed to be a romantic evening for me and my friend. We went out with her local friends, who happened to all be boys. The deal was this: before the end of the night I would have to be kissed by a boy, period.

I had just turned eighteen years old, I had never had a boyfriend, nor had I ever been kissed on the lips. She wanted to fix me up with a boy from her friend group, and I had to kiss one of them just to feel what a kiss was like. I wasn't desperate at all to kiss somebody. I found the whole thing so funny. After dinner, my friend and I started dressing up. I think that was the best part of the night. I was having so much fun trying on clothes that I could have never worn at home: a tight black lace dress, black Converse, and a small sporty purse. My hair at the time was under the effect of my first big chop, so the curls were getting natural and bouncy, even though some straight hair was still present on my head, due to the chemicals I was so used to putting on.

My friend was in charge of the makeup because I didn't have a knack for makeup. I remember her putting eyeliner, a little bit of mascara, and a bit of lip gloss on me. I don't recall if I had any foundation, but the overall look was very simple, and in hindsight very easy to achieve. I also had put my contacts in. I looked bomb, really cute. The dress I was wearing was hers because the only outfits I had brought were oversized and nothing feminine or slim that could enhance my curvy figure, which I was so ashamed of while growing up.

I wanted to look like her and my other friends, who wished they looked like either Victoria's Secret angels or Brandy Melville's models, posing like sorority girls in pastel-tone pictures. My body in high school looked very different, depending on what year I was in. During my third and fourth year of high school I was underweight, reaching almost 44 kg (97 lb.) for 1.63 m (5'3"). I didn't have a medical condition, but I was on the borderline that thankfully didn't go toward other spheres.

When we went out, I felt these were the things I wanted to incorporate into my lifestyle: going out with my friends, living close to the beach, meeting up with boys and with my girls, and just having fun. Again, I wasn't even looking for any romance. I knew that I wanted to have these kinds of moments in New York too, but that was a dream that would come true way later. Not much later though, just a year or two. Anyways, back to the memory. When we were out in the streets, I spotted something new. For the first time I saw the looks I was receiving from people, and even if I were feeling pretty good about my appearance, I could see that my "exotic" look was playing a big role in the scene. Before meeting up with the boys, my friend and I decided to go for a drink. She was with a boy from her friend group and I was paired up with one of this boy's friends. I didn't like him. I think he didn't like me either. Basically, we were going out on a double date if we can call it so. But I wanted to keep with the challenge.

While we were waiting for my boy to come and meet us up at the seashore, we stopped at a bar and ordered a drink. Well, my friend and her guy ordered a shot for all of us. I didn't know what a shot was, and little did I know what absinthe was. I took the whole shot just like a glass of water, with such a nonchalant and classy move, trying to emulate the moves that I was used to seeing in those old Hollywood movies: a glass of brandy in the hand of some actor like Marlon Brando, a pose like only Audrey Hepburn could do, and a piercing, captivating Marilyn Monroe-like stare. I burped and choked loudly as a reaction to the pure absinthe that I had taken in. We all laughed, me included, but from that moment on absinthe has been triggering to me. My date arrived, and my friend and I, along with the boys, hung out with other local youngsters. Before going back home my friend and I parted ways for a few minutes. I found myself alone with my date, who kissed me on a tree log in a parking lot while we were waiting for my friend and her date. Since we had parted in opposite directions and my phone connection was low, it took us almost an hour to get back together to go home. I remember my friend was mad at me because I had taken too much time and I was trying to make her understand that my phone's reception was bad. We didn't sleep well that night because the vibe was a bit off between us, but the next morning we smiled at each other. Our challenge was complete. We spent the following day at the beach, laughing, talking about how dorky my kiss was, and just commenting how these boys from this provincial small town were compared to the ones we used to hang out with in the city, in Florence. That night my date was already hanging out with two other girls and had forgotten about me. I wasn't sad, but I was disappointed. I started wondering if it was because I wasn't wearing the same makeup as the night before, or if my hair wasn't contained enough.

When our other friend arrived, we all decided to go out at a guy's place who was having a small gathering with his friends. The evening was nice, nothing crazy happened. However, I recall that night as "the green lipstick episode."

At the news of the presence of potential boys open to a quick hook up, my friends made sure to dress up for the occasion in a special way. After my first kiss, I was done with boys. I really couldn't care less because part of me already knew that among the three of us, the boys' attention would go all over my friends and not me. Despite these thoughts, I placed my self-esteem on a higher level that late afternoon, and I was sure that a second kiss would come. It happened all the time to my friends and in the movies, so why should it be any different for me? Come on, a girl can dream. That evening I decided to put my new green lipstick on. I had bought the glossy lipstick in Florence before departing for the beach with my friend. When I put it on—very hideously, since I was really bad at makeup—everybody thought I looked horrible. My friends weren't enthusiastic, but they said that it didn't look bad either. I was just trying to replicate a Rihanna look, a kind of visual that nowadays is considered popping and fashionable, even at a workplace. When we arrived at the guy's house, all the boys refused to look at or talk to me. They started pointing at me and my lips, my hair and some of them started commenting about my body shape. When we started playing spin the bottle, everyone refused to kiss me because of my lipstick.

Their comments were my first experience with racial micro-aggressions, which I had never had the courage to speak up about, and never had I recognized them as such. I just thought that I was ugly, and for this reason no guy would actually be interested in me. How could it be that this look I had made—even if not perfectly applied—was famous and liked by thousands of people on Instagram, from where I had taken inspiration for that night's look, and not in real life? Was I really that different from these Instagram models who literally looked like me?

The following month, I tried to pull this look off again in the USA, and I had mixed responses to it. Did it look horrible because I had put it on incorrectly, or because they simply didn't find me attractive? This green lipstick episode opened my eyes. What was the reason behind me trying to emulate this look I had seen on social media and in fashion magazines? Because the girls who wore this kind of lipstick were Black girls, with an urban look that I found so cool and wished to replicate. But I had forgotten that most of the eyes that were going to be upon me were white eyes, non-American eyes, provincial eyes. "The green lipstick episode" opened my mahogany eyes. Now I could see the style I wanted to portray whether people like it or not. I had two choices: avoid pursuing my style, or fully embrace it. I slowly went for the second option.

From "the green lipstick episode," I started digging into more fashion. I wanted to see what more was out there in the realm of what seemed to be unreachable or non-replicable.

When I arrived at college, fashion was still not a topic of interest. It all began when people would describe my looks and the way I would dress up for classes. First, I wanted to be like Blair Waldorf, sticking with a classical Audrey Hepburn look.

Then I switched it up to gym clothes, looking up to American celebrities like Teyana Taylor, Kehlani, and some Instagram influencers based in the NY metropolitan area. Then Ariana Grande entered the game, and surprisingly, that changed me. Ariana Grande was a link between Italy and the U.S., like the soft connection I had.

She helped me to be smoother with this transition. With her style I was able to maintain my Audrey Hepburn look, but also experiment with other styles that I wasn't able to showcase in Italy, without judgement or harsh comments from my peers and family.

Ariana might be small and tiny in stature, but her impact has been anything but petite in the fashion industry. Apart from her successful music career, Ariana has a versatile style, which can be divided into two macro groups: a pastel-colored feminine one and an urban-clean minimal one. Baggy shirts and pants are a must in Ariana's closet. She displays her femininity in various ways, by always portraying the idea of an innocent grown-up woman, yet full of life and with a big heart.

Her style is a marketing strategy, no matter what you might think of her. She knows how to market herself while being comfortable in her trendy looks. On the other hand, she has also developed her style through many pastel doll-like dresses, tight at the waist and large at the hips. Considering her physical appearance, Ariana tends to wear short dresses and skirts, paired with long, knee-covering boots or chunky sneakers. She also had a ballerina phase, but that seemed to have been more of a teenager thing to do. Ariana has a lot of influence, and her editorial campaigns are a big success every time she collaborates with a fashion house. The same thing goes for music personalities like Billie Eilish, Lana Del Rey, and Cardi B, who, thanks to their musical acclaim, have been major targets for brands and fashion houses.

However, to answer the question "What's your style?" I never answer with a label or a fixed terminology that helps me describe the fabrics, designs, and manufacturers of the pieces. I tend to get more philosophical and touch the meta of things, going beyond the physical sense. Comfort is the best style, and whatever I'm comfortable answering within that moment, I'll go with it.

HISTORY OF FASHION

My first approach to fashion began with my passion for biographies, especially those of Audrey Hepburn and Marilyn Monroe. I didn't take any fashion courses, nor attend any arts or fashion institutes. I'd say that my first touch of fashion happened because of, first and foremost, Audrey Hepburn. How I came across Audrey Hepburn is interesting.

In 2006, my mom took part in a TV game show called Mercante in fiera. In this show, the contestant had to play the homonymous card game and the winners would get up to 200.000

euros. One of the songs in the intermissions' soundtrack of the show was "Breakfast at Tiffany's" by Henry Mancini, from the movie with Audrey Hepburn, Breakfast at Tiffany's. Every time that song would come on, I'd ask my dad to turn up the TV volume. For this reason, one day my dad surprised me with a DVD of Breakfast at Tiffany's. He suggested that I watch it, but he also had told me that I probably wouldn't get it. I began learning English by watching movies.

I remember watching Breakfast at Tiffany's, and just as my dad had thought, I didn't grasp much from the story. I was only enchanted by the music, the location (because it was New York), and Audrey's pose. "How delicate and cute she is," I would think. My dad hadn't told me who Audrey's character was, or how complex and somber some of the themes were in that movie. I relied a lot on the visuals. That's how I fell in love with Audrey Hepburn. My dad was practicing his English with the same method I was using, watching movies. Given his age and his love for old Hollywood action movies, he suggested another movie for me to watch: the iconic The Seven Year Itch with Marylin Monroe. Different from Breakfast at Tiffany's, Marilyn's movie was easier to follow because of its plot and idiomatic expressions. In this way, by the time I was in middle school I had developed a great passion for the 50s and 60s, even though my knowledge was limited; I'm affirming this with a hindsight perspective.

Marylin's life was so captivating, but not relatable with mine. The more and more I started reading about Audrey, the more familiar I became with her biography and anecdotes. Her life was the first celebrity crush I had. I was in awe of her life, almost obsessed. I was struck by her strength, how she was strong during the Second World War under the Nazis' invasion. I looked up to her because she had the courage to move to another country and ended up in the United States, while always maintaining contact with her motherland, Holland. Her passion for chocolate, romanticism, dance, and kids were things that I could see myself with too. "One day I will find love and have a family and be a Tiffany's ambassador. I will work as a writer, but I'll be fashionable and gentle and poised and lovely. I'll be a Black Audrey Hepburn."

Well, that is my story of how I entered the fashion world via books and movies. The beginning was very home-schooled and self-made, as you can imagine.

When it comes to the history of fashion, scholars explain the evolution of the marketing of fashion, including how garments and shoes, in addition to accessories like hats, gloves, and jewelry, have been constructed with designs and cultural backgrounds. Political history and geography play a big role in the history of fashion. Since fashion is a pragmatic form of art, it is, consequently, a clear reflection of a certain society or population. Fashion has always existed, from the very first moment men and women decided to cover their bodies to keep themselves warm.

However, fashion as a form of art is pretty much a new thing. Charles Frederick Worth (1825–1895) was one of the first designers to sign his name in the labels of his clothes. Before Mr. Worth, clothes were mostly sewn specifically for the clients who would come to a fabrics store. This was accessible to few, though. Most people, either in the West or East, would make their clothes inside the household. Creating clothes was in fact a domestic chore, predominately done by the women of the family.

A historian I like to follow online and learn from is Shelby Ivey Christie, a fashion and costume historian I came across on Twitter. She gives daily impressions and views on the state of fashion, but she also provides a large database of academic resources with which readers and followers can inform themselves on a huge spectrum of fashion issues and themes.

One of the most interesting tweets she has ever shared was one related to the history of dandyism in Congo, by mentioning the phenomenon of "La Sape."[2] There's a documentary called The Congo Dandies: Living in Poverty and Spending a Fortune to Look Like a Million Dollars by RTD that describes this extravagant lifestyle dominant and proper in the Democratic Republic of Congo.[3]

Another tweet of hers that sparked my attention was the one related to Marie-Thérèse Houphouët-Boigny, the first Lady of the Ivory Coast from 1962 to 1993.[4] As Christie points out in her tweet, American media used to refer to her as the Black version of Jacqueline Kennedy, especially after her visit to the White House in 1962. This fact made me think and pushed my thoughts beyond the label of "Black" and "white." If we think about it, there are still a lot of fields, companies, and career paths that still feel the need to enhance the importance of highlighting the presence, the promotion, and the

---

2 Shelby Ivey Christie, Twitter post, June 29, 2020, 9:53 a.m.
3 Natalya Kadyrova, The Congo Dandies: Living in Poverty and Spending a Fortune to Look Like a Million Dollars, Video.
4 Shelby Ivey Christie, Twitter post, June 20, 2020, 2:50 p.m.

comparison between Black people and white people. Why do we need to keep hearing and reading the same headlines and phrases that put us non-white people, especially women, in a place of comparison? Why are we so limited to the color of our skin? Don't we have a separate identity? Marie-Thérèse Houphouët-Boigny is different from Jackie O, as much as the Congolese dandies come from another experience than the British dandies like Oscar Wilde. The history of fashion needs to shine more light on different personalities and realities, with a large spectrum of shades and hues.

I could write a whole book on the history of fashion, from the Egyptians to the Italian Renaissance, from the Greeks and the Romans to Princess Sisi's times in Wien, Austria. I won't load you guys with dates, facts, and every single trend you could think of, but I will tell you the most important phases that modern fashion has gone through in the Western world, at least those that I know. When it comes to the history of fashion, I usually just analyze and dive into the story of one garment or one accessory. Let's take, for example, the jumpsuit.[5]

The jumpsuit was one of those remarkable inventions made during the early twentieth century, a period when creativity and pragmatism would often go hand in hand and serve each other. Jumpsuits were created by a Florentine designer who went by the name Thayaht (Ernesto Michahelles) in 1919. His design, initially thought of as an everyday item, became so popular among the Florentine socialites that it sparked an interest in other cities and luxurious environments. The "tuta" (the original name of his jumpsuit design and the Italian

_____

5   Maude Bass-Krueger, "Vogue's fashion encyclopedia: The jumpsuit."

translation) started to gain popularity among women and other strata of society when in the 1930s another Italian fashion designer, Elsa Schiaparelli, customized this garment for women. Throughout the following decades until the late 1970s, the jumpsuit was considered an elegant piece, versatile and slightly casual, malleable for any kind of activity and occasion. The jumpsuit had its first editorial debut in the Vogue September issue of 1964. When celebrities and fashion houses started showcasing the jumpsuit, with patterns and accessories of all kinds, this item became as fundamental as the common little black dress that any fashionable wardrobe should collect. Along with the little black dress, jumpsuits are one my favorite fashion items I dearly care about. From the history of the jumpsuit we can learn a lot about the history of women, feminism, sexual intersectionality, and pop culture. Think about how androgynous women can be while wearing a jumpsuit. Think about how masculine, sporty, classy, and edgy a man looks in a jumpsuit. The comfort, the versatility, and the modernity of a jumpsuit is timeless.

I study fashion by taking one item at a time and dissecting any aspect it carries within pop culture, art, politics, and language. But I am very much aware that a lot of fashion history still needs to be surfaced, to be known, and emerge from its archives. I need to learn more, and I'm super aware of that. But hey, Fashion on the Beat is my open letter, statement, and affirmation that I have found my beat. Now I have to compose the melody. Let me dive in.

French fashion was the first milestone with which fashion had established itself as a career choice. In the 1920s and 30s France was the greatest nation for fashion houses, followed by

Germany, Italy, England, and Spain. Between the 1940s and the 1970s, fashion found its spot in society. Fashion was consumed by the masses, even though it was still a very elitist aspect of society. The 40s and the 50s saw brands like Dior, Chanel, and Balenciaga take off and become the trendiest among the wealthy. In the 1950s, after the tragedy of World War II, fashion witnessed two directions: one kept the traditional vibe, the other one started printing more and more social statements. This was the reflection of the societal classes arising, and the youth wanted drastic changes. The 60s and the 70s were solely focused on and managed by the youngsters, making fashion a space where sexual liberation, expression, and comprehension were possible to execute. From this period, I always recall Yves Saint Laurent, one of my favorite brands and designers. The 80s and 90s until today have seen fashion becoming a homogenous, worldwide lifestyle. Women can be more androgynous, and men can be more feminine. We are witnessing a mix and match, and I personally am enjoying all of this.

WHAT TRENDS ARE WE WITNESSING?
THE FUTURE OF FASHION

I see a future in fashion, a thriving one. Fashion has a more tangible sense of entrepreneurship. Fashion is accessible to anyone and is a lot more expressive. Fashion has entered and is part of the collective imagination, and as a part of our lifestyle. However, the structure with which we can access fashion on a professional level is still very strict and rigid.

When I visited Atlanta in the fall of 2019, I got in touch with a bunch of people in the creative community. I was able to visit vintage stores full of stylists, designers, and experts in the industry. I realized it was more than art: it was business, a dealership, the art of communication, quality-searching, and style-hunting, all with the same objective: make a less negative impact on the planet while keeping the love for fashion alive.

To be a dedicated journalist, your eyes must be attracted to everything, and your ears should catch every beat of information around you. Sure, you can skim and choose what's important for you to focus on because news is just like what we eat: there's junk food, fake food, mediocre food, and tasty food. I try to follow a healthy diet, with which I can have all the necessary nutrients and my favorite dishes in a span of twenty-four hours. Throughout the day I usually stick to a plant-based or pescatarian diet. But when it comes to the mornings, I allow myself the privilege of having a savory breakfast.

Savory breakfasts change from time to time. They give me the chance to mix up my palate, leaving it intrigued and ready to appreciate unexpected tastes. However, life gets in the way. Sometimes I don't wake up feeling hungry at all, and I just drink my protein shake. There are times where minutes are essential, and I need to spend time in front of the mirror instead of the kitchen table, so I grab a quick small package of cookies and run to wherever I need to go. I just accept it, digest what I have, and report the facts. The life of an aspiring journalist, as they say.

During the last four years, my breakfast routine has dramatically changed. Before college, breakfast was a timed moment, where homework and my telephone didn't have much significance. Once I moved to Hofstra, a new set of environments were part of my breakfast scenario. First, the cafeteria. Second, the classrooms, where some professors allowed us to have breakfast in class. Third, the desk in my room, which I shared with three other roommates. Fourth, on the way to classes, on the sidewalk, sometimes on the subway, the train (countless times lol), or on the bus.

I've realized that the way I'd consume breakfast would automatically affect the ways I'd digest news. Before college, I had newspapers, TV, and my dad exchanging conversations with me. At that time in my life I was passive in receiving, sharing, or commenting on the news. Afterward, I was on my own and I had to rely on my own eyes and perception of reality. I needed to shape my vision of the world without voices suggesting to me what to think or do, like my parents would—as any parent does. At the beginning it was hard, especially to confront and understand bigger institutions and corporations in another language, but with practice and patience I could see the results.

The more I got to know my surroundings and figured out what I wanted to learn from my college experience, I started being religiously attentive toward the news. However, I was following just a limited number of channels and platforms. When I began approaching the news hand in hand with my classes and other extracurricular activities, and cutting off unfulfilling friendships to expand my professional and personal networking connections in the city, I found some pleasure and necessity in keeping up with the news.

If it wasn't for my interest in civic engagement, fashion modeling, and entertainment writing, I would've never gotten deep into the real purpose of my goals and dreams: writing to advocate, to represent, to be a bridge between communities, while being in contact with the beauty of the visual arts—the dream of an aspiring journalist.

Social activism is bittersweet. Activism has good intentions tarnished by capitalistic profits that a typical Aquarius wants to dismantle, along with challenging situations that push and question your privileges. In the fashion industry, social activism plays a big role, but not many people see this side. Fashion is a Gemini; it has two faces. One is glamorous and the other one is full of complications and rewards, confrontation and victories. And you can understand this only if you're a news junkie, only if your intellectual diet includes all the nutrients of the culture.

For this reason, I've started appreciating a savory breakfast whenever I start the day. What a weird analogy to compare food with media, right? I need to remember the sweet and the bitter of what this world has to offer me daily. Not only do I have to know this with my intelligence, but also, I have to stimulate my body to be receptive of these facts. The only way to prepare for such a lifestyle, one proper of a full-time journalist, I must exercise my palate and digest some salty and sweet. Maybe one day I'll change again and go back to having only desserts for breakfast. Or maybe I'll just stick to salty food and limit the sugar. Who knows what kind of journalist I will be? I hope to stick with the bittersweet kind, a balanced one.

Maybe it's the New York tradition, but a poppyseed cream cheese bagel with a glass of fresh orange juice, or a cupcake with a glass of almond milk, or a bowl of cereal with fruit salad on the side, or a cup of green tea with two slices of whole wheat bread and eggs is an ideal breakfast. A bit of salt and a bit of sugar. A bit of CNN and a bit of Twitter. Some Instagram scrolls and some e-mails: the balanced and realistic breakfast of a journalist, at least an aspiring one, in search of guidance and success in tough times like this one we're living.

Now, time for breakfast. What are you having? Just remember to drink water!

PERSONALITIES AND MY PERSONALITY

Trendsetters around the world change every season for different purposes. They get along with what sells the most and what is trendy or not, creating the influencer culture that we millennials and Gen Z youngsters are very much used to. However, a couple of distinguished trendsetters' styles and role modeling have been in the game for some time and have great potential to expand and be more and more significant. I will mention only the top seven from my list, but that doesn't mean that the others I consider great role models in fashion are not equally remarkable. I just see a global impact from the individuals I'm about to mention. Their work isn't focused on fashion only. They use fashion as a social justice tool.

With the events of the #BlackLivesMatter movement and the white guilt that it's highlighted more and more these days, people are giving astute observations regarding the state of the U.S. Police brutality has existed since the foundation of this nation, along with colorism, racism, and economic inequality. In addition to that, people are getting educated and they're trying to find answers to any questions raised.

Despite the mobilization and the massive spread of news online, people still have jobs to do. There are people—editors, chiefs, CEOs, presidents, etc.—who need answers that stand out in a neat and polished way, no matter what emotions we're going through.

These days I find it very hard to answer calls and messages from my friends and acquaintances, especially the Italian ones. I am glad to exchange information, educate them on what is happening here in the U.S., learn from them what they think about the news, but I would lie if I said my heart didn't shrink when I talked to some of them.

I was speaking on the phone with one of my best friends, who wanted to know more about the protests and my well-being, but he was also asking some questions that I found absurd. Another one laughed at my articles and thoughts. The list goes on, and my feelings are heavy and mixed. Sometimes I'm disappointed to be surrounded by negative and narrow-minded people.

After these conversations, I realized that being an Italian POC based in the U.S. during these times brings a lot of experiences and knowledge that you might take for granted, but in reality you need to explain carefully what's going on here. To put it simply, sometimes my mindset is more American than Italian or Brazilian. And I'm coming to the conclusion that I'm not the only one experiencing this. A lot of Italians (especially those who have lived here longer) do share my concern.

You can't assume that people consume news and share the same experiences, directly or indirectly, within your space.

The week I moved to my first apartment after college, I realized I was having real adult conversations. It hit me right in that moment. My voice matters. My points of view can be a deal breaker and can upset people. My feelings toward a heated argument need to be calibrated, especially as a journalist. There are no rights or wrongs, but there are places a person decides to stand.

Now more than ever, it is hard to have different kinds of talks with non-black people, especially with those who have never lived in the U.S. and never had my skin color or heritage. Basically, I'm living as a baby, someone who knows her stuff but needs to mold her space in this world.

A lot is going on. A lot needs to be balanced and evaluated. I learned that I'm no encyclopedia to anyone, I don't have all the answers to my white friends, and even if I'm brown, I need to get educated on several issues too. Speak up and pick up a book. We need to pull UP for ourselves in our own space. UP!

I know where I stand, but I recognize that I need to work more on how to deliver my passions, especially since I am not from the U.S. As much as I'd love to work in a Black, Latino, or non-white publication, some topics need to be supported by evidence, opinions, and feelings solely from an African American or non-white American perspective. My real journey as a journalist, writer, and young Brown woman has officially started.

I've graduated, but school has just started: the school of life. Just like my peers in the industry, I am expected to engage in conversations in a certain way. Sometimes I still feel behind, but I've become comfortable with this discomfort of mine because I've trained myself to find any source and material right away as fast as I can.

CHAPTER 2

MODELING, ENTREPRENEURSHIP, AND OTHER VENTURES

―――

Girl posing, making a statement
Wish I could look like this girl, a fearless and bold
young woman.
Outspoken.
She's young. She carries a lot of colorful shades in her
puffy "curlylicious" majestic hair.
Black is beautiful.
I would love to be similar to this girl. Because she's
brave. She owns her femininity, she's warm inside and
spreads lightness.
Black girl magic.
Fit as strong.
Gentle as easy.
Light as bright.
Kind as refined.

A concept blooms. I close my eyes. I see it,
me dressed up, visually satisfied
my hair all up, a full crown
my face washed up, a canvas for my teeth
I would paralyze, sedate, kill any fear inside me so that I
could look like this girl, the girl in my concept.
Goals.
I open my eyes, switching off the app. I stand up, put away
my phone, take a pencil.
I am sketching a sharp future version of me – a caring
cosmopolitan delicate woman.
Keep hustling.
Keep inspiring.
Keep listening.
*Summertime sadness (a mood), by me, and not Lana del Rey,
while scrolling down on my Instagram feed*

THE ORIGINS

Memory is both a blessing and a curse. There are times
when I wish I didn't remember some episodes that
occurred in my life. Some of those events were hurtful and
unpleasant, which brought me a lot of pain. Even though
these moments didn't have any joyful significance, I am
glad to know that I am able to reminisce about them. The
benefits of comparing the past and the present moments
in your life help you stay on track with your personal
improvements and goals that you want to achieve in the
future. I try my best to keep track of my memories. For me
it's an exercise, just like yoga. I keep track of the places I
was in before checking other ones. I think about the past
to live mindfully the present. I can define and understand
myself in this way.

The most significant moments in my life happened in the summer. I don't feel old enough to write an autobiography, so I'm not going to bother you by explaining about my life since day one. I have a blog for that on my website, thecurlyflower. com. However, I will refresh your memory, or if you've just come across me, you can learn the basics of Giulia. I was born in Bagno a Ripoli, a province of Florence, in 1997. I stole Cupid's day, and he punished me with a big curse: being a bitter, hopeless romantic, in love with the idea of love. Yes, I was born on February 14th. My mom recalls it as a sunny and bright Friday morning. I don't believe much in astrology, but I'm an Aquarius. Most of my friends are Pisces, Geminis, and Sagittarians. What does it say about me? You tell me.

I was raised in Florence, by a caring and lovable mother, and a caring and strict father. I choose to differentiate "lovable" and "strict" respectively for my mom and dad. See, my mom has always been a solar presence in my life. My dad has been too, but I had more resistance toward him during my teen years, even though when I was little, I was such a daddy's girl. I started appreciating his strictness just lately, during my last two years in college. I guess that's part of life, especially for a woman. I love my parents equally, and I cannot stress enough HOW much I love them. I would be lying if I didn't tell you that I often get mad at myself because I wish I could give them the world like they were able to give a whole universe to me. I am sure that day will come, when I'll give them the best gift ever, the best vacation ever, the best of the best of the best . . . Well, you get my point.

I'm an only child. I get mad when people assume that only children are the most spoiled ones. In some cases, this is true, but in others it is not so true. I stand with the latter. My closest friends can affirm this fact too, knowing how my parents raised and educated me. Related to this thought, I should mention my very first vivid memory.

I believe I was four years old. It was a feijoada. For those who don't know, feijoada is a Brazilian stew made of black beans, beef, and pork. Feijoada is usually served with white rice and farofa, a toasted flour mixture that tastes like . . . farofa. If you get the chance to try it, please do. It's so good. That's what I say now, because when I was little, I didn't like feijoada at all. To the chocolaty eyes of a four-year-old, feijoada looked too spicy and hard to handle. Fast forward fifteen years, my tongue reevaluated that thought. My parents would host a feijoada lunch once a year between November and December.

They would invite family and friends and share with them a big meal that my mom would meticulously cook for days before the actual lunch—especially the pernil com abacaxi, a typical Brazilian Christmas dish. We had guests from different parts of Italy, Asia, and America. Before moving out, our Japanese neighbor would always attend our parties and play the piano with my friends from kindergarten and elementary school. She was an exceptionally gifted professional pianist.

That year, in the early 2000s, we had invited many guests, and I was wearing a red dress. The house was filled with kids, music, food, and smiles. I remember going back and forth in our corridor greeting guests. I remember I was happy. My first vivid memory that pops into my head is a Brazilian party in an Italian house, with family and friends.

I remember also spending my first vacation in Brazil in Rio de Janeiro when I was five years old. Technically, that wasn't my first trip ever to Brazil, but it was the first I remember. I was with both my mom and dad. I remember the music, the joy, and the love, along with my family members and their close friends. My Brazilian family is big. I wasn't used to having big family reunions back home in Europe. For a long time, I've been living in a dual world, exposed to both large and small companies made by cousins, aunts, uncles, and grandparents. I get the best of the two worlds. Another memory I recall is the time I learned how to clean and cook shrimp at my grandma's house in Porto Santo Stefano, in the south of Tuscany, where my dad is from. Cooking with her and playing on her balcony with her colorful plastic clothespins was so fun. In my fictional world, they were tiny people living in the city, a.k.a. the balcony. Fun fact: the city I would always imagine was Los Angeles, specifically Hollywood because the house faced a hill and from the cartoons and movies I used to watch, the only cool place I could think of was Hollywood with its iconic white sign.

My dream of coming to the U.S. started at a very young age. I don't remember exactly what pushed me into this idea, or why was I so determined to spend some time away from home, but I believe the influence of my mom's story and my dad's job had a great impact on me.

My parents met in Switzerland. Years before, my mom had left Brazil for an au-pair job in Germany. She lived with her aunt, who was based in Switzerland at the time along with her spouse. My mom lived between the borders of these countries for a couple of years and took care of two little German siblings. In a heartbeat, my mom learned German through an intensive course and practiced her English daily, with almost no contact with Portuguese speakers. She met my dad at a party. My dad came from another reality. He was doing his PhD and completing his post-graduate studies, just before being hired by the University of Florence. He fell in love with her. She fell in love later. When they both synced, she visited Italy. My dad went to Brazil and asked my grandparents, my mom's parents, for their daughter's hand. My mom moved to Italy. They got married. Five years later, here I am, born on the day of love. Hearing this story was one of the coolest things I remember from my childhood because it was a story full of airplanes, car rides, two continents merging together, different places, climates, and cultures, all of them gathered in the name of love. "I will have a cool story like this too. This looks fun. I get to travel and find a prince charming. I can't wait for my time!" I would think.

However, the only country I was exposed to since I was little was basically the United States. I didn't care if it was New York, Kentucky, Georgia, or California. All I could think was, "These are the places all the kids in the movies make their dream happen. This is where my dolls come from! Barbie goes to Malibu. I wanna go there too!"

Little did I know that almost two decades later I would find myself in the country of Barbie and Ken, the Bratz, and Disney Channel Originals. And little did I know that fashion and journalism were going to be part of my life.

FROM MODELING TO WRITING

Modeling made me understand the marketing side of fashion, where you see a product's visual and concept on a body. The art of modeling enables the display of an idea, which in fashion is a garment made with different materials, shapes, and colors. However, the core of fashion stands in what the models wear. What am I wearing? and, maybe more importantly, what do my clothes say about who I am?

I made it to college with my average pear-shaped body, big curls dominating my head, and round blue Tiffany glasses on my face (I lost those glasses on my way to a photoshoot, can you believe it? I still can't. lol). For the first time, I saw something I was missing back home: diversity. In fact, at college, I was surrounded by many Black and Afro-Latina girls, whose hair and faces were like mine. "That's it, I found somewhere I belong," I thought. However, this was not my community. I am not an African American woman. I'm a woman with Afro-Brazilian roots who grew up in Italy. I can't fully relate to African American history and events. Am I an Afro-Latina? Well, I don't think I'm a Latina because Spanish is not my first or second language. So, who am I? Again, these were questions that only with my friends, and later during my junior and senior year, could I find answers to in both an academic and personal setting.

So, it is not difficult to think that for me, when I came to college, seeing girls who looked like me and were more than just a small group was a triumph. In hindsight, I consider that reaction naive and innocent, merely because my life had not yet exposed me to life-changing experiences where my mind, heart, and spirit would be questioned and challenged.

For this reason, fashion was the most welcoming way to get into this new world of diversity, where I could find myself while learning from other cultures. I found a way to express my own heritage, my personality, and my mind through fashion. I discovered myself in that space and community, after years of low self-esteem and mental health issues. Yes, throughout high school I had mild obsessive-compulsive disorder, something I had to find out about and cure on my own. Through fashion, I was able to enter the world of social justice and representation on my terms and capabilities. With fashion I learned to appreciate other people's beauty. With the right mentors, readings, and meditation exercises, I learned to navigate all aspects of beauty.

I must say that I bumped by chance, very randomly, into the profession of modeling. It took me time to understand my worth and how to see myself in the industry. I raised both my hand and my voice to ask people to guide me and help me understand if this could be a real career option. My destiny is unclear no matter how strong my determination is.

As I became more entrenched in the day-to-day world of the fashion industry, I began to view the sustainability of the industry differently. I would say to myself while browsing my closet and wondering what to choose: "Do I really need this t-shirt? Why is this bag so important to me?" Lots of questions that had been suppressed for a long time suddenly became important, and my perspective on how the world works shifted yet again.

The facts made me question my ethics and behavior toward fashion. Different people and magazines reported that it takes almost two gallons of water to produce one cotton t-shirt. Most of the clothes we wear are made from plastics. According to the Environmental Protection Agency (EPA), "The total generation of municipal solid waste (MSW) in 2017 was 267.8 million tons (U.S. short tons, unless specified) or 4.51 pounds per person per day."[6] Can you imagine those numbers now, in 2020, and beyond? Is my passion healthy for others? What exactly am I participating in by purchasing these things? I decided to investigate and apply my journalistic skills to explore one specific side of fashion: fast fashion.

After reading Elizabeth Cline's The Conscious Closet, I expanded my knowledge in fast fashion. The author not only explains what fast fashion is (which I will explain later in chapter 4) and is becoming, but she also proposes detailed ways how fast fashion can be reduced and reevaluated. It's a non-fiction personal narrative in the world of fashion.[7] I was inspired to commit to sustainable fashion, a colorful scenario in which thrift shops, vintage clothes, and resale stores are the protagonists. More on this will be in chapter 4, with Kenny's interview about the vintage business and Tamara Jones on sustainability as a lifestyle.

Fashion can be malleable: it's not only a visual experience, but it can also be lived by listening to the words of the experts, members of the industry, and music. Hence, the title of this book. The benefits of fashion and its studies reside in their mobility. Fashion is dynamic, but to follow

---

6   "Guide to the Facts and Figures Report About Materials, Waste and Recycling | US EPA."

7   Elizabeth L. Cline, The Conscious Closet.

it you need to be disciplined. Fashion taught me to be clear in my intentions. It gave me a view of the world from the inside, where I could witness the injustices and be vocal. I could use my position of both fashion model and writer for the world.

MODELING: FASHION MODEL AND BUSINESS MODEL

A model is a person who wears and poses for an artist. Models can be found in the visual arts, with painters and sculptors, but the most famous ones are those in fashion. Being a model is not easy. They need to follow a specific healthy diet, they must exercise, and their schedules are full and hectic. Being a real fashion model is complicated, it's a whole commitment that few can accept.

The fashion industry is the most iconic when it comes to complexities and dynamics in the world of job-searching, coworkers, start-ups, and collaborations.

The fashion industry is a complex one. I mean, every industry is full of complexities inside, because it's a world we live in now, full of intertwined systems. Everything we think of has the potential to be a marketing strategy or a profitable outcome, especially in capitalistic societies. The fashion industry benefits a lot from capitalism. Costs of production and high demands of consumption requires a fast economy and the ability to foresee the likes, dislikes, and needs of the majority. Fashion is a fluid industry since it involves so many disciplines. Think about psychology. In order to entertain and attract new consumers, the fashion industry spends a lot of money and time researching trends and what exactly people appreciate in their wardrobes, what they would be willing to purchase to fulfill their dreams, and what they would do to have a certain style, both with or without a limited budget.

Think about finance. Making investments in fashion is a real thing. For many entrepreneurs it is a solid and a secure move to invest time and money in brands or fashion companies. What fashion can offer that many other industries don't is flexibility and creativity. These abilities have a great function in fashion and you can have them without actually having an academic degree. However, no matter what kind of education or diploma is achieved, being educated and having communication skills are at the core of fashion. Within the industry you must be able to deliver your messages with details and knowledge, culture and discipline.

When you want to be in fashion, you must set a goal for yourself. You need to understand that everything is a business motif for your work, and most of the people there want you to eat less at their table. It sounds harsh, but it is like that. The cliché from the movie The Devil Wears Prada is somehow true.

Andrea Sachs, played by Anne Hathaway, assists her evil and cold boss, Miranda Priestley, majestically performed by Meryl Streep. Andrea strives and looks up to one of the most influential fashion editors in the world, while Ms. Priestley fights her inner devils. From this movie, many of behaviors and attitudes of the fashion world have been seen properly: the dumb models, the hectic studios, the frivolous behaviors of the stylists, designers, makeup artists, and the ultimate strict, heartless, and stubborn editor in chief. However, as in everything and in every person, fashion has a good side and a bad side, and a somber part in its most glamorous part. You can approach fashion at any time in your life. Fashion isn't an instinctive thing for many, but a lot of people who are not creative get into this industry because they see the benefits fashion can give them on a personal and career level.

FASHION IS THERAPY, AND WRITING ABOUT IT IS TOO

I can see you picturing a slim and tall young lady walking in her shiny stilettos, nails done, shades on, and a bright red lipstick, strolling around a big metropolis with big paper bags on her arms. This image is one of the fantasies in the world of fashion. It'd be like saying that all public relations workers act or look like Samantha from Sex and the City. You might wish it, but that's not the case, my dear. This image is a pure rarity and an abstract idea of what being in fashion or media is actually like. Besides the chaotic and fast-paced rhythms that these fields have, there are also some advantages. In this section I will share my opinion on why fashion is a therapy, and where we can find healing practices within the spaces the field provides us.

Fashion is meditative. For me, being on sets as a model was more an enjoyable activity rather than an exhausting one. One thing taught in meditation is the importance of being present and the ability to give and receive the present at any given time. When you are on set, you are asked to be focused. You need to cooperate and make your body available to be the canvas of the project. You must know what you're doing and mindful in your purpose. When modeling I would ask myself: "Why am I doing this? Am I just helping this brand, earning money, being part of my friend's project, or is there something else beyond these thoughts?" If you want to get into fashion, you must recognize that the dynamics of such a world are demanding. But you need to learn how to place yourself into the companies you work for, especially as a model. You have to know what's happening around you. It seems like you don't have any time to rest because a lot is happening at once in different parts of the world and in many parts of fashion: style, cosmetics, beauty, fashion shows, new companies, and designers rising. Fashion might drain you, but it also gives you the possibility to live the present moment at its finest, by just writing and discussing issues that can be solved in the instant they are out, by suggesting new ways and visuals that can make a huge impact and change people's lives. I think that fashion is meditative because it has the capacity to put you in an uncomfortable position, and it is you who must promptly decide to make a fast change, with a meaning and purpose. Doing so is a difficult task, but the outcome is thrilling and gives you pride.

Working with images is part of what the fashion industry deals with too. As we know from psychology, images, colors, and shapes play a great role in our psyche, making us think and react to certain situations based on what we see and perceive. Human nature is primarily sensitive to what is superficial, so humans tend to trust more with their eyes rather than with their mind. In fact, it is easier to rely on a present feeling rather than going through an analysis process and picking a side, product, or style.

Fashion can be a form of therapy too. If you need to heal from a trauma or a difficult phase of your life, fashion can help you do that. The variety of colors and mindsets that members of the industry create and publish is escalating more and more. In addition to its creativity, fashion is an open business that can be connected to many ventures, and it is able to give you enough space to think about yourself and your work. Timing might be the only challenge that the industry has, but once you've got your project and ideas all together, fashion is fertile soil for your concepts to flourish and have fun with them, while making a profit too, sometimes.

Last, but not least, fashion has a social representation purpose. This aspect of fashion is still on its journey to being established, but it started in the late 70s and 80s, with fashion models like Naomi Campbell and Naomi Sims, but also with personalities like Coco Chanel and Yves Saint Laurent at the beginning of the century.

Nowadays being a fashion model requires more skills than just the physical ones. You don't actually need to be taller than 5 feet and 7 inches, have a pretty face, and a slim body with a sculpted tummy. You can proudly embrace your natural, healthy body, but you must carry a mindset that is strong enough to carry and go after certain narratives. Models today showcase clothes, accessories, and ideas because of the industry, the society, and the life we currently lead. Everything we own reflects who we are and who we aspire to be, especially the latter.

A MODEL WHO WRITES: MIA

The stereotype of finding tons of models on social media is true, mostly on Instagram. In this way, thanks to social media, I came across Mia Yarborough. What struck me about her was her beautiful hair and lean figure, which captured my attention along with the work from her modeling portfolio. In addition to her modeling, I found her humor, as well as, her lovable character, which turned out to be empathic and genuine like mine.

As a model, actress, and poet from Baltimore living in Los Angeles, Mia explores her passions through the power of the pen, by writing feminist and intimate poems that embody her visions and personality.

I took some time to ask her a few questions about how she sees modeling from an artistic point of view. Nowadays the position of a model on set is much more respected, and there are times when the models themselves must collaborate with a brand's or show's production.

- What does modeling mean to you?

Modeling has been a love of mine for almost my whole life. I started when I was ten years old, and over ten years later, I have fallen more in love with it than ever. Modeling was always a way for me to create art, and I used it as an outlet when I was going through very hard times. It was my escape. For those few moments, I could become a different person, and it felt freeing. Now I use my modeling as a way to express the woman that I am today. I like to experiment and do interesting concepts. I love to play around with masculine and feminine roles and just be who I want. Modeling is more than a career to me, it's my world.

- Do you think that creative writing can create a meaningful impact in fashion? Can you create a photoshoot/ editorial out of a poem?

As a writer myself, I definitely believe that creative writing and fashion can go hand in hand. Writing an amazing and well-thought-out creative piece means you need a lot of detail, and if you use those details and turn it into fashion, you could easily come up with a beautiful new concept. I personally could turn a lot of my poems into photo shoots that will either encompass the mood of the poem or focus on a certain line or idea. I believe all forms of art can easily be brought together to bring new life into it.

- What's your love of fashion? How do you explain this passion for fashion?

I love that fashion has no rules. You are able to express yourself freely and openly through your clothes, shoes, jewelry, etc. Fashion is, like I said before, art, and I really admire those who can create crazy new concepts and wear them so proudly. Fashion is so much bigger than just streetwear and fast fashion brands. There are so many creative designers and individuals who can look at a piece of fabric and create something out of this world, and that is why I love fashion. It's limitless, there are no rules, there's no right or wrong. Yeah there can be judgment but so what? Fashion is an expression of the soul and that's just another thing that I love about this whole industry.

- Is fashion exploring new ventures, according to you? Do you think the industry could do better in incorporating new media?

Fashion is all about taking risks and exploring new ideas. There's no fun in everyone wearing the same thing or dressing the same way. The industry could definitely try investing in new ideas and media, especially from younger designers and designers of color. Every day I see new, talented, and amazing designers on my Twitter or Instagram, and if they were given the chance and the right resources these young people could make a huge difference in the fashion industry.

- Last but not least: define fashion in your own words.

Fashion is an art form, a way of life for many, and an outlet for people to express who they are.

IF YOU WANT TO BE A MODEL, KEEP IN MIND
PLAN B, C, AND Z: IT IS WHAT IT IS

If you're reading this book it means that you were lucky enough to be chosen by Mother Nature to be on Earth. You're reading these words because you got the chance to be educated, and that's a privilege. Maybe you're reading this book because you're hoping to get all the answers in order to get into the fashion industry. When you picked this book you probably thought that I was eventually going to go over the trends and what makes you pretty enough to be on fleek, hip, and cool. You might want to know what it's like to be a model, or how you can get into modeling. Well, all I can say is you can actually be a model, and you can make it into fashion as a model. No doubt at all. Nowadays you don't have to show how pretty you are, but mostly how wonderful and mesmerizing your mindset is. Your rules must be out of the box. Get creative and inspired by any means. Being beautiful has no rules. Beauty is a social construct. Being pretty doesn't mean much of anything anymore in the fashion industry. It depends on the country you want to work in, their standards and sociology. Beauty is complicated. I want to report beauty in my words. However, if you don't make it as a model, don't beat yourself up. And if you do reach and pass certain steps in the modeling industry, don't make any dumb moves that might jeopardize your job.

Consider modeling as a job in the arts. You have no guarantees that you will secure your bags, your stability, or connections. You must come up with a plan B and more. If you've got yourself, whether there's a camera in front of your face or not, you'll always be a model—a role model to yourself.

Again, since I still consider myself a baby in the making, with just one foot in the fashion industry and one hand in the journalism field, I can share my interests and experiences that might serve you in the future. You can take as much inspiration as you want.

Considering my body type (height: 5'5," weight: 110 pounds, shape: pear) and my main occupation (student/journalist), when I was offered collaborations and fashion shows participations as a model, I got more interested in taking a shot and maybe pursuing this as a full-time career. A part of me didn't want to do it because my main dream was to be behind the cameras rather than in front of them. Nevertheless, my curiosity never failed me, and an inner fire was burning to know more about this possible adventure. I was blessed to meet many models, women and men, who shared with me their takes and stories in the industry. I saw models striving. I saw jealousy, I saw envy, and I saw hate. But I also saw a lot of love, collaborations, and community initiatives. One of the people who shared information with me is Alyssa.

PIVOTING AND BEING YOUR OWN MANAGER: FROM FASHION TO ENTREPRENEURSHIP WITH ALYSSA

Entrepreneurship is not a common thing in Italy. At least, it is not as flexible and accessible as it is in the U.S. Or maybe it's not a popular topic at the center of many conversations among young Italians. One of the reasons why I came to study in the U.S. was due to this factor. My family has always pushed me to look farther than my local options, and the U.S. seemed to be the best place where I could start thinking about my future while getting a higher education. We never thought about the aftermath, but the dream to succeed in the U.S. and experience the American Dream was something that my family gave me the option to take. I took it. I've lived it. And now I'm a totally different person.

I both lost and found myself in the USA, with the American Dream. I knew what it was, but I didn't know how to live through it. Arriving here was like living a dream at first. When I was nineteen years old, my first and foremost desire was to get out of Italy. High school wasn't one of the happiest times for me, although I have beloved memories in my mind. In hindsight, I wish I had maintained high school friendships, but I've learned to let them go.

Distance hits you hard and an ocean makes the difference, no matter how helpful the existence of Skype, Facebook, Instagram, Twitter, or WhatsApp is. I've arrived at Hofstra with the burning appetite to grasp everything that I could in order to do the only thing that I've always wanted to do—write. Even if I was sure about my ambitions, I didn't know how the system worked. I was an A/B student in high school, very focused, and the geek in class. Boys didn't like me, and popular girls didn't click with me much. I had very few friends, with whom I've made unforgettable memories. Among the group, I was always the most cosmopolitan one: half Italian, half Brazilian, with an American Dream in mind. Again, just in mind. I would get all my information through movies, pop music, and literature. Journalism wasn't a thing swirling in my brain. For this reason, the things I knew about America were a small percentage, filtered and partially misrepresented. I wasn't aware and prepared to work in the system.

However, we go to school to learn, right? College has been such a formative experience. Given my interests and thirst for knowledge I craved, the first years were a full exploration in communications, where I learned tons about self-expression, representation in media, social justice, and ultimately, journalism.

The last two years have been focused solely on how to work and be present within the system. Dealing with bureaucracy, understanding rights and laws, learning the business lingo, getting internship rejections, and getting modeling gig refusals was super hard at first. In the last phase of my academic career I've decided to finally embrace my creativity and make something out of it, at least start thinking about it as a business, a lifestyle, an income, and a generational practice—my American Dream.

During my first year at Hofstra, all my attention was focused on my academic grades and my life on campus. I needed to adjust to this new lifestyle and the only thing I had clear in my mind was to get along with the environment surrounding me. Even though most of my time was spent on campus, I would walk and explore the Big Apple. I would visit the Lower East Side as well as Greenwich Village and the SoHo area. No matter how comfortable I was getting in wandering around the city by either myself or with my friends from campus, I was missing the nightlife and the European lifestyle I had back home. Sure, I wasn't the girl who would go every weekend to the disco or chill out at the bar at the local corner, but my mind craved moments like these. In the U.S., kids cannot drink before twenty-one years old, and for me there was no appeal in getting drunk, wasted, and stoned at parties. My second year in college was difficult because a lot of my friends were changing habits and interests, and I couldn't find anyone who wanted to do the same things as I did. I started using Bumble and similar apps to meet people to just hang out. I didn't like Tinder because it scared me, and never will I use it (again), but that's another story for another book.

Spring 2018. I was tired of being stuck in Long Island. Living in the suburbs was an experience that changed my life, but if I had the chance to go back in time I would think twice about living far away from an urban setting. Being on social media hurt me a lot during that semester because I was scouting a lot of art events, art gallery openings, and so much more, which I couldn't attend due to classes, money (for transportation), and distance. Growing up with a mom who's an artist in a city like Florence, those kinds of events were so familiar to me. Every creative in Florence would meet each other at these functions and parties. When I was in Italy all I could think of was coming to the States and applying that kind of lifestyle here. Now that I'm here, why do I still have to wait? Why are there so many limitations? Why are there other people my age who get to do this and not me? And just like James Dean, I became a rebel without a cause. There was literally no apparent cause for me acting this way, but in hindsight, I can see what happened to me: I wanted to live and I was tired of obeying one institution, one lifestyle, dictated by the trends of my friends. I wanted the luxury and the glamour of Carrie Bradshaw and Serena Van Der Woodsen from Gossip Girl, but Black. I wanted to be part of that Black Girl Magic movement in the city of my dreams, but I couldn't do it on campus. I was tired of waiting.

One night during that semester, I cried so much and had my first real panic attack. My grades weren't very good, my motivation was under my feet, and the boy I had liked for quite some time had refused to be in a relationship with me. In addition to that, I was missing my friends back home, my family, and my best friend who I had lost contact with the previous year. That was my first episode of loneliness and depression. I couldn't think straight, and I didn't have one little ounce of self-esteem. I was just sad, disappointed, and tired of feeling like I was never enough for school, people, and myself. I've always been hard on myself, but that was one of the most remarkable times. I had put a lot of blame on myself for things I couldn't even control. I didn't know how to love myself, even though I cared about me and the people I loved. In this confusion, I could only cry, cry, and cry. A lot of people were telling me to just start sleeping around with all the boys who found me attractive, drink my problems away, smoke and do other stuff that I had no interest in trying. I thought I had problems for being interested in cultivating long-term relationships and interests without smoking or drinking. I spent that night in my dormitory lounge on the thirteenth floor, cuddled up to my knees while staring out the windows until the sun came up in the morning. I barely slept three hours, and when I was dressed to go to classes something inside me clicked and turned on a button I didn't even know existed: rebellion.

Just out of the blue, I decided to ditch my classes. I remember it was a gray, rainy Thursday. I had a little money I had saved the previous weeks, and with that money I was able to buy two tickets, back and forth from Mineola and Penn Station. I went with no purse or bag to Penn Station. When I arrived at the World Trade Center, I called my friend Maddie who lived close to Battery City Park. I went to her place and together we decided to go to Brooklyn. That night changed me.

I met Maddie at an art gallery in the Lower East Side with a collective of collage artists. We exchanged numbers and social media accounts, and we kept in touch throughout the weeks. When I explained to Maddie my situation and the reason I was crying, without thinking twice she invited me to spend some time at her apartment. This moment looked like a lot like that time I had ditched my homework to go out with

Isa and her friends back home in Florence. In addition to that, while I was walking to Maddie's I stopped at H&M to buy a dress for the night. I bought a $10 dress which reminded me of the dress I had worn the night of my first kiss. A lot of these subtle details pushed my subconscious to rethink about some memories I had either suppressed or forgotten while I had been so busy adjusting to a new life in college. Finally, I would have fun again on my own terms, just like at home.

That night wasn't my first time going to Brooklyn. The first time I had been to Brooklyn was in 2015 with Coco, in Williamsburg. This outing with Maddie was at night, though. For the first time I could go out, probably drink a little bit (I was twenty-one at the time and even though I'm not a drinker, I enjoy some alcoholic sips from time to time—no beer, please!) and get loose without having to think about grades, homework, assignments, and school drama. Maddie and I went to this party, which I ended up finding out was just an open mic night, with rappers, queer artists, some models, and even nobodies with no labels or anything, like me. I met Alyssa that night. Alyssa was with her best friend Victoria, who had approached me in the crowd. She recognized me because we had met at Hofstra the previous year. Since our encounter had been so brief (not even ten minutes), I thought I would never meet her again, and I was surprised she remembered me. We had no idea that a couple of months later we would become roommates. For this reason, through Victoria, I met Alyssa.

Alyssa is a commercial model represented by EMG Models and the CEO of her digital company Booked 'N Busy. As much as my other friends who have been guides and mentors to me for both my life and for my career, Alyssa is such a dynamic individual whose projects float from one point to the other with the same rhythm and flow she applies to her life. Her goal is always to empower women and feminine energy with constructive dialogues that rotate in being financially independent, stable, and secure. From her experience and point of view, I wanted her to explain her business and her thoughts on the fashion industry. She's a real one, and she speaks without sugar-coating the facts. If you want to know more about her work, go check www. bookednbusy.org.

- What's Booked 'N Busy?

Booked 'N Busy is a digital platform and real-life community of millennial women who are interested in amplifying their mind and their money and learning how the two are intrinsically linked together.

- What does financial freedom mean to you?

To me financial freedom means being able to access the things that my heart truly desires without having a limitation on it. Financial freedom means not only giving myself freedom and access to those desires, but also providing that same sense of freedom to my friends, my family members, and my communities, and encouraging them to reach financial freedom as well. Financial freedom is not stressing about how much is or isn't in your bank account. You just live life freely because you're comfortable with where your finances are, and you're able to give back in ways that you never dreamt of doing.

- How would you define your experience in the fashion industry? What did you learn and explore there so far?

From the fashion industry, I learned that you have to be extremely comfortable and confident in your own skin. You can't allow other people's perspectives or opinions of you to break you down. What's most important is how you feel about yourself. External perspective and views of you don't determine your self-worth. You determine your self-worth.

- How do you manage your life as a model and an entrepreneur?

While my life as an entrepreneur is much more predictable than my life as a model, as an entrepreneur, I'm able to create my own schedule that aligns with the goals my business has versus being a model. I'm on someone else's schedule. I can be called to last minute castings, and I can book a job the same day. It's very up in the air so you have to have more flexibility when entering the modeling industry as an entrepreneur.

- What are the real talks that nobody knows about in both these businesses?

I don't think everyone knows how much work it actually is until you start doing it. Typically, you're a one-person show in the beginning. And who knows how long the beginning actually is. So, it's a lot, a lot of work, and you need to have a good amount of self-discipline. And you have to be passionate about what it is you're doing in order to persevere and in order to continue going out of strong momentum on your entrepreneur journey/business idea that you have going on as a model. One of the things I feel isn't spoken about as much is not everyone is getting paid. Yeah, there's a lot of money in entertainment, modeling, acting, and the related industries. But not everyone is booking jobs. You can go months without booking a job and if modeling is how you've decided to earn income and you have no other side hustles going on, you could be broke for a couple of months. There could be one month where you book a $5,000 or a $10,000 job. So, it has its ups to it, but it does have its downs. It just depends on what the industry is looking for, what's trending, who audiences want to see, who they are looking at the most, and it's less about your personality, and it's more about your physical appearance solely with modeling for someone who wants to start crafting ideas around entrepreneurship.

- Do you have any platform you consider valuable to start crafting ideas around entrepreneurship?

I would definitely recommend Girlboss. They have a great digital platform. They also have a networking community where you can connect with other like-minded women or not only like-minded women, but women who can challenge your perspective in the best of ways. I think Pinterest is really good to serve as like visual inspiration. I feel like Instagram is great too for another good platform to craft ideas. You can see what other people are doing, and better yet, you can see what other people aren't doing. And if someone's not doing something that means it could be a great business idea for you as long as you do it the right way.

- What do you plan to see in the future? Any fresh business models or topics we millennials and Gen Z should be keep an eye on?

In the future, I plan to build my business and my empire, and my empire consists of multiple packets. It's not just one avenue, it's going to be something bigger and greater that all leads to one common why.

SO, CAN I BE A MODEL?

In the past, I had one toxic trait. I used to compare myself to others, and it wasn't because I wanted to be pretty or successful. In high school, I wanted to be accepted as I was, but only a small group of people were willing to get me. I've always wanted to be seen and talked about for my brain, never for my looks. I always thought I was a bit ugly, you know, the geek girl, but I was never a sad kid. My shelter was my home library, where I had access to books. I could travel back and forth in my imagination, and that was enough to me. However, my toxic trait of comparing myself to others came up during my junior year in college. Let's start with a statement here, right now: everybody is beautiful, and nobody is beautiful. I grew up in an environment where Black or brown women were not the subject of likability. In the U.S., I found out almost the opposite. Whenever I used to question my physical beauty, I found (a bad) refuge in thoughts that would go like: "I was left and dumped by all of them because I don't look like these ones, I'm not exotic or wild like them, I still go to school, I have a baby face, etc." And honestly, that was the worst thing I could've ever done.

My very few friends who supported me during these times of extremely low self-esteem—after a failed friendship, a romantic relationship, or an academic downfall—said that this behavior was legit because I was hurt and genuinely sad and I was missing being important to someone and society, but this kind of reaction was the worst one to choose, even though the easiest one to be dragged into. Wishing to look like someone or blaming is easy. I thought I didn't have any right to feel happy, loved, or interesting. All the things I cared for and loved seemed to fall, and I deserved to not be happy anymore. I was bursting with ideas, but I couldn't execute them. So I felt discouraged to go on, and I just wanted to stand by. Basically, I was deeply depressed. So yeah, my temporary solution during this time of confusion was to compare myself to others, especially to other girls in the fashion industry. And it's been some time now since this toxic trait of mine has dissolved. And whenever it comes back, I give myself a pep talk. So, I came up with a new mantra:

"You are you. You can't be them. They are they. They can't be you. It is logical. 'You' are you. They are 'they'. Close your eyes. Are you in your body still? Good, so you are still you. Deal with what you have. Your body is yours, and you gotta make it work for you because the only person moving for you is you. You are yourself. They are themselves. They got what they got. You've got what they don't have. You can appreciate what is up because you've been so down. You've felt alone, but never lonely because you have you."

This philosophy has helped many friends of mine and made me rise more and more. They could see my confidence, and they could be more confident. They were happier and willing to listen to me more because they would feel more apt to approach me (I tend to isolate myself a lot when I'm sad). I'm writing this because someone who feels down can actually benefit from these words. I know how it feels. If you need to, read those words again as if it were a math problem. When you feel and love tons you gotta read and think shit in the straightest way possible. And damn, that changes things! You even love more. But a better and clearer love comes with this behavior. Love for yourself and for whoever/whatever. And these positive thoughts got me more into modeling and appreciating this form of art.

HOLD ON, THOUGH: CAN I BE BEAUTIFUL, OR AM I ALREADY BEAUTIFUL?

Mother Nature gave us great bodies. Our bodies are diverse, and with them we can do many things. When our bodies aren't that simple to move with, they push us to engage other activities and mindsets that force us to be punctual and positive in our lives. Give thanks.

I wasn't given the gift of being tall or super skinny. I'm not even thick or voluptuous. Still, I give thanks to the universe for what I have. My height pushed me to focus on one kind of modeling. My body structure and skin made me realize how rich and inspiring I could be with my diversity amongst different communities. And my perfect/imperfect body gave me the chance to explore my writing, making my hands the most powerful tools I could ever use. Hence, my love for fashion and journalism with which I could express myself through the art of writing and glamour.

I'm telling you this, dear reader: I learned to fully love myself the moment I embraced the fact that I needed to nurture everything that I liked to do, including crafting my intelligence and heart, the most personal and special things in my persona. I'd rather pay attention to what I think, love, and believe in with a specific intention. I can enter a room and make an impression without looking fly AF. And that's the sexiest attitude I can have in any industry, especially the fashion industry. It may take time, but my heart will always be full, and that's key. Once I've tasted the flavor of freedom, I couldn't go back. This empowering, positive, and energetic feeling is too scrumptious to resist.

Am I pretty enough? Yes. Because the world is full of pretty girls, and honestly, everyone is gorgeous. Do I have enough luck? You do because you're healthy. If you have health, then you have everything. If you have a roof, then you do have some privilege. If you have the capacity to love and inspire others, then you do have some power in yourself. Working in the fashion industry made me realize the pretty sides of my body and appreciate them. If I don't like something, I can embrace its differences and create a genuine narrative around it. Fashion forced me to understand and take my privilege into consideration. As a light-skinned, multilingual, biracial young woman living in NYC, I've experienced a lot of envy and jealousy from girls and boys in the industry and on campus.

When sad people see you happy, they can do the weirdest shit to bring you down, especially when you're out there for the sake of love and passion. However, my focus on fashion taught me that through my small privileges, I can inspire others instead of being judged by people I shouldn't pay attention to. Everything I do or say must have a purpose.

So yes, I believe that I will make it. I don't know how. But I'll be ready for any change while keeping my focus constant and tight. I'll keep surrounding myself with only the right number of people and skim the bad news in my life's timeline.

I talked about my experience and what I am living right now. But these are words dedicated to everyone, especially girls, who feel like shit because I've been there, and there are days when I still feel that way, even though I pick myself up pretty fast. Who feels lonely and far from family and friends? Who has lost a person they loved a ton? Because this time last year, I felt like I had nothing to give to the world. I wish I had come across words like these. So, if you're sad: it's going to be better when you're tired of feeling sad, giving with no receiving, or existing but not living.

CHAPTER 3

FASHION JOURNALISM AND MY PASSION FOR WRITING

———

A boy meets a girl.
they swirl
like snow
they burn
like sun
they pop
like blooms
they fall
like walls.
-*just a meeting*

Dear readers,

Explaining America to Italians is both difficult and easy. Common places and stereotypes can help describe some realities. Yes, buildings reach the sky. Yes, rappers do have a lot of tattoos, and most of them are African Americans. Yes, guns are legal and streets in California seem to never end. Just like in the movies, you know? Just picture that and you've got it, more or less. And that's when the challenge starts.

In Italy we're taught American history from 1776 to the 1970s, until Watergate. Between these dates, we don't even get the chance to explore much of the issues. We study and learn from the Civil War (1861–1865), World War I (1914–1918), the Roaring Twenties (1920–1929), the Great Depression (1929–1933), World War II (1939–1945), and the exponential economic boom (from the 1950s to the 1970s). And even among these periods, we know a fact or two that were the keys to move forward to the next phase closer to our contemporary times. Sociology is not taught, and demographics are not at the center of our schools' tests. We know what the American Dream is, though. The American Dream is the concept of ultimate freedom and independence, protected by the law and the culture. But it is one thing to know it, and another thing to live it and form yourself around this idea.

In 2002, the European Union "devised a multilingualism policy whose goals were to: (a) raise understanding of the EU's linguistic diversity, and (b) to provide all citizens opportunities to learn two languages in addition to their mother tongue."[8] Having this mission in mind, learning foreign languages in the European Union isn't fresh news, yet the

---

8   Farahnaz Faez, "English Education in Italy: Perceptions of Teachers and Professors of English," 34–35.

reception and the practice of it has changed throughout the decades. "The first half of the twentieth century revealed a sense of 'hostility' toward English and Americanization, the second half of the century showed signs of 'accommodation' and 'acceptance.'"[9] As a country filled with rich and intrinsic traditions, Italy and Italians are extremely proud of their culture, and any sign of innovation and integration is taken slowly. This fact explains why "books, movies and other resources generally get translated into Italian thus contributing to a lower level of need and desire for knowing and learning English."[10] The laziness in learning something new comes from the mere fact that our communication services are sufficient inside the national borders, and provincialism is still a reality.

Despite this general remark, Italians are interested in learning English because of their attachment to mainstream media and in order to have better and more employment aspirations, they make sure to learn and practice the basics of the language. Technical English—especially in the fields of art, fashion, business, and electronics—is advanced, but the levels of comprehension are not refined when it comes to literature, academia, or the entertainment industry.

Public education in Italy is free and mandatory until high school, and it has a centralized management. Differences among regions exist, but in general English is required to be studied beginning in kindergarten and until the end of high school (which lasts five years).

---

9   Ibid., 33.
10 Ibid., 39.

One might argue that the Italian educational system provides programs that enhance polyglotism, but the quality of teaching overall lacks consistency and variety. Learning the grammar of multiple languages can be easy but having the ability and possibility to speak and practice two or more idioms is a skill that only polyglot people can actually perform, and even enjoy doing. Standard English is the only medium Italian students get to explore, whether it is British English or American English.

One instructor interviewed by Faez says that the system shouldn't focus only on "teaching more like grammar-translation methods in which you only teach grammar and how to translate" because "it doesn't really help people to communicate."[11]

My experience of learning English reflects a particular situation that often occurs in Italy. Biracial and immigrant families tend to spend more time and money in making their kids learn English in separate institutes, workshops, or international schools. The majority of these families are from anglophone countries that were former British colonies (Sri Lanka, India, Nigeria, etc.). In my personal case, my family decided to put me in additional English school—first a British institute, then an American one—because they wanted to prepare me for a possible college experience, which happened years later. English was not my second language, nor did I speak it regularly at home. Despite this, my exposure to the language was empowered by the media (music, movies, and books) and family friends from the UK, the U.S., and some

---

11   Ibid., 40.

from the Caribbean (mostly Jamaica). At school I would mostly learn British literature and standardized grammar. Real conversations where I would test my communication skills were held outside the classroom.

The multi-purpose functions that the English language performs in academic settings have various roles, outcomes, and consequences for those who are both learning or teaching it. English is one of the most known languages around the globe, even though English only slightly surpassed Mandarin Chinese. In 2019 there were 1.27 billion English speakers, whereas the Chinese were only 1.12 billion according to a study conducted by Statista.[12] Regardless of how many people speak or understand English, the methodology with which English is taught isn't heterogenous like its audience is. The way English is both instructed and absorbed by non-native speakers has different repercussions in media, politics, and ultimately in contemporary lifestyles.

Being able to learn a foreign language should be considered a privilege that allows one to explore a culture and a society external from those we were born in. Min-Zhan Lu's piece "Silence to Words: Writing As Struggle" gives an insight of what it is like to learn English while growing up in another country, with a different language and political philosophy.[13] The ability to teach a language is a professional achievement that must be performed with an attitude that is open to curiosity, comprehension, and cultural exchange. This kind of approach is found in the rhetoric of American

---

12   Niall McCarthy, "The World's Most Spoken Languages."
13   Min-Zhan Lu, "From Silence to Words: Writing As Struggle," 437–448.

scholar Jamila Lysicott, famous for her TED Talk video, "3 ways to speak English."[14]

However, it is not always easy to teach the English language with its rich vocabulary and myriad of expressions. There are several contexts that make this process difficult. Learning English is often a tortuous academic journey that immigrant students or even young native speakers face on a daily basis, due to the presence of outdated legislation, in addition to racist and elitist realities that go hand in hand with the society we live in.

Standard English and institutional regulations, on a federal and national level, make the English learning/teaching process more difficult to deliver and perform.

I think that my experience as an international student of color in a predominantly white university has shaped my language and perception of communication. My heritage has played a great role in this aspect and had a huge influence throughout my college career. Many times, I felt different or even excluded from social and academic settings, due to my accent, grammar usage, and the topics I wanted to discuss.

I will always be a learner in this country and English will always be my third language. For this reason, I am invested in exploring both its customs and trends. To engage in such an activity, I must recognize and analyze how the politics around the English language work, the regulations that enable a certain type of teaching, and how to communicate

---

14   Jamila Lyiscott, "3 ways to speak English," video, 4:06.

with other immigrants. My experience is as unique as many others, and I am glad to have been taught English in different scenarios. I feel relieved I was able to absorb other American English dialects and idiomatic expressions, which allowed me to deeply understand practices like code-switching, making me more aware of my surroundings and the behavior of certain people.

COMMUNICATION IS KEY

My passion for fashion was born out of love. It came across just like an unexpected love story, full of ups and downs. They say true love comes from the heart. From the heart you can take both love and hate. And when it comes to fashion, I can see both the good and bad in this world. The spectrum is generous and vast. In order to keep this love story of mine with fashion, I had to learn to communicate. Communication is key in every relationship, even when it's you and your career, work, and passion. You must find punctuality and purpose in in your interpersonal verbal skills.

If you want to communicate in this world—a fast, dynamic, stressful, and pixelated world—you have to know how to live in the present, in the moment. Being present in your communication skills is fundamental. Being present is important for yourself because you develop a speech delivery that will enable you to move both freely and independently in every topic you'll discuss. Communicating is great because you don't feel alone. If you know how to put your thoughts out there, you'll always be able to attempt an integration in every conversation you come across, and you'll never feel simply left out just because you didn't open your mouth.

In my case, I have found fashion the medium and topic that eased me to speak in front of crowds, friends, and family. Through fashion I can form an opinion around all the issues and events happening around me. Sometimes it's not easy to approach journalism. To understand my approach, you must know my story and a specific episode that struck me and changed my life.

When I was four years old, I wanted to be a classical ballerina at Teatro Verdi in Florence, a small but very elegant theater close to my house. I viewed Teatro Verdi and its majestic rooms and stages as the epitome of success, and at a young age I was dreaming to show how my body was able to make gentle movements in pretty dresses and relaxing music. However, my dream to be a ballerina faded away pretty quickly because all the ballerinas I knew didn't look like me. I also didn't like pink as a color, and so I felt discouraged. I couldn't see myself wearing pink clothes all the time and couldn't imagine my hair brushed like most of the ballerinas I knew—little white girls. I wanted to be part of something that could speak to me. I wanted to represent, but how was I able to do that if I wasn't represented? I was a hyperactive kid, very smart for my age, but also sensitive and creative. Later, after many attempts at choosing what sport or hobby I could do after school, I stuck to swimming. I loved to swim because it made me feel free, and subconsciously I always longed for tropical places. So, when it was winter in Italy, my anti-depressive shelter was the swimming pool. I was lucky enough to have found great coaches, especially one during my high school years, and a supportive group of friends, my teammates. Even if it was an individual sport, I loved swimming as a collective experience with some of my best teammates. But no matter how great the environment I was living in, I knew that I was different.

My hair, for example, was difficult to manage. I've always felt uncomfortable wearing wool hats that shaped my hair in such a weird way that it made me look like a mushroom after every training session. My skin was always ashier than the others' because the chlorine in the swimming pool was more visible on me than on my other friends. My hips were always bigger than the other girls', even though I was very slim, almost at my lowest weight I've ever been (97 pounds and 5'4"). I had big curls, curvier hips, and more melanin in me. From time to time some girls of color would take part in the swimming courses, but I was always the one struggling to put the swimming cap on alone. Despite these difficulties, I embraced my differences and realized how unique I was. I didn't perceive them as a struggle. Maybe it was because in my family, between my mom and dad I never experienced any big racial issue or event that damaged my immediate family. However, I cannot say that racist events didn't occur either. In fact, I never had real talks with my mom about being Black, biracial, or anything else, not like the majority of Africa-American kids who are used to navigating these topics. I would have these conversations with my Brazilian family, but in Italy this was a rarity. I'd never suffered from it, but it definitely bumped into my life later when I came to the U.S.

When I came to study at Hofstra University, I only knew one thing: I wanted to be seen and heard through my writing. And I didn't want to study math or science. Well, I still had to take math and science classes, but the dream to write was accomplished, and it's still in the process. I knew I wanted to write, but I wasn't sure how and what to write about. I felt like coming to New York just to write movies or romantic comedies was a bit of a waste of time. "I could've done this at home, or I could've moved to Hollywood," was what I was thinking at the beginning of college. During my first year of college I had the chance to explore all the academic and extracurricular clubs that the campus offered. Because of my background in Italy, I had put tons of high expectations on the college system. I thought it was a place where I could experiment with everything that I wanted to try, express myself, and find my path in writing, whatever kind of writing career I wanted to do.

My repressed and hyperactive childhood phase came to the surface during my first year in college. I literally put all my energy in finding out what my passions were and where they were. I tried to dance, but that didn't end well. I still enjoy dancing but the groups my college offered didn't make me feel comfortable. Coming from Italy, hip-hop is not very well-known, so the first group I tried to be part of kicked me out. I felt like they didn't have enough patience to teach me or make me feel included. I was a bit sad, but I didn't give up. I tried many writing workshops and slam poetry events on campus, and those made me feel included. Artsy people and social activists were the communities I was more engaged with that would listen to me, and mostly importantly, I could learn from. All I wanted to do was to get in touch with people because I didn't want to feel alone, and I wanted to be seen and inspire people. I knew that if someone could see me and I could inspire them, then ultimately, I would learn from those experiences and interactions.

In my sophomore year I was asked to choose, once and for all, my major. My parents also were low-key expecting this decision. Being an international student isn't simple because you don't get much flexibility in deciding what you want to do or explore, given the bureaucracies and the investment that your family has made for you to study and live in another country. In some ways I felt that I needed to get back to my parents and finally choose what I was doing, in an official way, on paper, at school. I was undecided between pursuing a career with only books or a path of studies that allowed me to be pragmatic and get creative with my knowledge. For a long time, I thought about majoring in drama, but then I picked journalism because I knew that I wanted to write movies, books, or plays because I didn't have enough confidence in my acting skills. I saw all these kids on campus who sang super well and were highly talented, who knew all the Broadway productions and movies. And in this cultural shock, I turned my attention to something that was a bit blander at first sight, but I could give it a shot. So, journalism came into my life.

When I was accepted into the Lawrence Herbert School of Communications at Hofstra, I wasn't sure if I had made the right decision. Very few international students were enrolled in the department, the kids seemed already professional and experts at all kinds of subjects. Some of them looked entitled, others noisy, and others elitist. College started to look more and more like a newsroom rather than a school. If there's something I must give credit to it is that department, and the simulations of real-life experiences, interactions, and duties that I got to go through. My experience was hard but thank you.

One day one of the students a year above me asked me what I wanted to do after college. We ended up discussing different kinds of journalism jobs because I had said that I wanted to become a journalist, if not a screenwriter. They made a harsh comment about the field of journalism I wanted to focus on, after I had told them that fashion journalism was an interest of mine. They said that fashion journalism wasn't as serious or relevant like hard news and the industry didn't need that kind of content as much as it needed political pieces. I was hurt for a few minutes, but then I took this comment in my heart and told myself that I could change their mind. "I'll show them how fashion journalism will be important, just as important as any other field in the media," I thought.

This was before COVID-19, Black Lives Matter, and all the other types of civil rights interests that fashion journalism has highlighted in its content. This was before Elaine Welteroth's position of editor in chief at Teen Vogue and before Samira Nasr was appointed as editor in chief at Harper's Bazaar. I still don't know what position I will ever have in this world, but I know that I am molding and reclaiming my own space in both the fashion and journalism industries, through my words. When I was in my James Dean phase, I was being rebellious without an apparent cause. However, I found a cause at the end of the day. I wanted to prove wrong those who told me that fashion journalism wasn't as important as other fields, those who couldn't believe that my English skills could improve (they're still in progress), and those who couldn't see me grabbing a pen, a notebook, and a laptop while being on a set or a fashion show. I needed to prove them all wrong.

FASHION JOURNALISM

To prove everyone wrong who thought that my choice of narrowing my journalism interests in fashion was silly, I decided that the only thing I could do was to get in touch with a few of my professors, share my thoughts with them, and do my own research with every instrument I could get access to. Journalists in the making use Twitter and LinkedIn, hence these two platforms served me as fundamental superpowers. I gave more attention to Twitter because I found a diverse community. I saw myself represented more in terms of race, interests, backgrounds, and skills.

One of the accounts I encountered on Twitter was Gianluca. Gianluca Russo is a featured fashion and culture writer, whose words appeared in publications like Teen Vogue, GQ, Glamour, and Nylon. He is also the founder of "The Power of Plus," a digital space dedicated to inclusivity and representation (you can find more at @thepowerofplus.co on Instagram). What drew me into Gianluca's page was his original content. Gianluca's area of interest is fashion inclusivity and visibility, especially in the male plus-size community. Another thing that attracted me to his work was his charisma and transparency online, something that I wouldn't see often at the beginning of my Twitter journey. Now that I had found my niche of people with the same interests, I had built the base of a strong space where I could get informed and relax at the same time. I had, in fact, carved my space and found the right people I could talk to about anything related to fashion, books, movies, art, and much more.

For Fashion on the Beat, Gianluca and I had a talk and he answered a couple of questions for me. I hope one day to meet him in person and thank him with a big hug for the motivation his pieces and his mindset have given me to continue to believe in my dreams when everyone else wouldn't do so.

- What's your background and relationship with fashion?

My first memory regarding fashion is when I was about eight or nine, and I was in elementary school and I was watching season three of Project Runway with Christian Siriano. Obviously, we don't know he's about to become a huge advocate for inclusivity and changes in the industry. And so, my first kind of exposure into fashion was watching him, you know, start to blaze this trail and win the show. And from there I realized that there were people within the fashion industry who wanted to make changes, you know, and who wanted to push for inclusivity in different ways. But I never saw myself as having the capability to do that, or the resources to do that, and so for pretty much my youth leading up to high school my, you know, mid-high school years. I always liked fashion. But I never would style myself because I just didn't have clothes in my size. And so growing up I always had that interest in fashion but it was never something I viewed myself as having a part of, until I got to the end of high school and I started to want to do more professional things.

- You're very prolific. You produce a lot of content and in a very confident way. And I try to read as much as possible because you don't see or read a lot of plus-size content or anything that is focused on that part of fashion, or that point of view. I would like to ask you if you ever faced any challenges in representing your beat or your topics of interest in publications and to editors.

I think in the past year, specifically, I have developed quite a spot for myself in this industry where I have some leverage to go to these publications and be able to talk to them about plus-size presentation in their editorials. What I found is that there are many brands that don't want to show size inclusivity on the covers. They want to show it in small ways, but they don't really want to take a clear stand, and so there is such a big market for pieces about plus-size fashion. There's so much to cover. And so that's kind of what I've devoted myself to doing and what I found is, obviously, that there's not many editors who are receptive to that. But even the ones that are, not all of them truly understand that. I view plus-size fashion with the responsibility of more than just clothing, because plus-size people have so long been kicked out of fashion and not given a spot in this conversation. There's a responsibility that comes with it because there's a message behind it, and that all editors understand that they see it as clicks. They see it as a potential viral post. And so, a lot of it is kind of navigating which editors care, and which ones don't. And so, I've been very thankful to connect with a good handful of advertisers who do care, and who do want to kind of continue this conversation and push it forward. And so what helps me now at the point where I am is that I can show them solid statistics and show them proof that pieces about precise fashion and putting precise people on your covers doing these editorials increases engagement and increases brand loyalty and morale.

- Where do you think your role in media is and what exactly is it?

My place in media is to push the boundaries to a point where maybe some people are uncomfortable, but where the plus-size community can finally start to see themselves represented in the way they have always deserved to be. There is a division in the industry where you can see the people who really want to push the needle forward, and those who don't. I view my position as someone to push them to the next step. That's what I try to do in every piece that I write, and that's why I pump out so many pieces, and we're always pitching new people and connecting with others because I feel that I have the position now in my career to be able to do that. And so, I always want to make sure that I'm always doing everything possible to represent plus-size fashion and concise people in the best light.

- Why do your write?

Everything I do, I do it for the impact. I don't write because I love to write, I don't write because I want to make money, I write because I want to have an impact on this community. Every decision I make, whether or not it gets me attention or followers or anything, I'm making sure that it's having an impact. And I think the most motivating thing to me is seeing that impact and seeing how my own experiences and my own voice can help others. And so I think the most useful thing for young people with these marginalized experiences is to see how they can use their personal journeys, their personal life experiences, and their personal points of view in order to help others and to shine a light on their own communities.

- What do you think about fashion journalism and the stigmas that are still attached to it?

I think for so long, fashion journalism was viewed as a frivolous thing; because for so long, fashion was only made for thin, rich, white people. So, it was viewed as an elitist thing and viewed as just clothing. But I think when we look at perspectives from marginalized groups, fashion means so much more than that. Because fashion has culture behind it, it has power behind it, and responsibility behind it.

- What is style for you? I love asking this question to any fashionista I come across.

I view style as a form of expression for oneself. I view fashion as the industry that gives us the options to choose how we want to dress, and how we want to express ourselves. And I view trends, as passing fate and passing phases that bring originality to the industry.

THINGS THAT COME WITH WRITING IN THIS NEW DECADE

COVID-19 has brought many thoughts and reflections to our tables and households. Jobs in the media industry are adapting more and more into online spaces, requesting a higher number of skills and qualifications. In a span of two full months, social media consumers have been also bombarded by news and trends on a massive wave. From high school students to middle-aged professionals, tons of individuals have been reevaluating their lifestyles and how they can sustain themselves. And in times like these is when fame can either be a gain or a jinx.

Good fame brings glamour into your life, and there's no one that can say the opposite. Being famous for your remarkable and talented services to the community comes with gratification. If you mess it up and do harm, you provoke an incompatible feeling with the collective audience you speak up to. Fame is a calamity that enters in private spaces, like with J.D. Salinger, the author of The Catcher in the Rye. Fame is also the most desirable blessing that a person could get, but it needs to be analyzed. Why do you want to be famous?

Last April, Drake released his single "Toosie Slide," along with a music video with the Canadian artist in his opulent residence. Comedian and beauty entrepreneur B. Simone launched her book, Baby Girl: Manifest The Life You Want. Kylie Jenner from the Kardashian family has purchased a $36.5 million mansion in Holmby Hills in the middle of a pandemic. Other celebrities and major media personalities show us ways to cope and keep our game up during such uncertain times.

For real though, how do we really cope, we human beings with no fat wallets, no permanent residence, no family, or partners close to us? We can all admire and seek our satisfaction through media and education, by reading and being inspired, but at the end of the day, how does fame play a role in our existence? Is there ever going to be a way to be inspired and reach fame, if it even exists?

When I was a first-year and a sophomore at Hofstra University, I was the social media manager of the Society of

Professional Journalists (SPJ) club. I liked that role because it allowed me to work with social media, and for the first time ever I had an insight of what being a social media manager meant. However, this wasn't the first time I had attempted to have such a position in a club. Months before joining Hofstra's SPJ, I was collaborating with the campus's fashion club as a social media manager. The experience started well but didn't end up being beneficial for me. Misunderstandings occurred between the board and me, and I felt my work wasn't validated enough.

Even though this very first experience didn't go as well as I had planned, during that first attempt of working as social media manager I had both learned and mastered social media skills, in terms of managing multiple accounts, figuring out algorithms, and scheduling a palette for the feed. With SPJ, I was able to create and establish a vision among my team with homogeneity and a collaborative spirit from my club mates. Working with Twitter, Instagram, Tumblr, and Snapchat for both a fashion club and a journalism club has given me a taste of different situations to navigate. At the beginning of my junior year I decided to resign my role and quit the club, and that was another first for me. I needed to see my work more validated, appreciated, and in balance with my mental health. I learned to say "no" to a position, no matter how much the perks or the job itself seemed appealing and in line with my academic career. My off-campus experience was very similar, even though it was very connected to my on-campus life.

Most of the time, my online presence reflects what is going on in my life. I started using social media to connect with my friends and family, without any marketing agenda. I've also used social media to recover from and cope with some of the most difficult phases of my life. I've never expressed an interest in becoming an influencer or to become an internet sensation or a trendy personality. I created a lot of visual content that was engaging and aesthetically pleasing. There are times when I look back and think that I could have kept that energy up, but once that happy period of life wrapped itself up, I felt lost and with no will to continue being myself. I was torn apart and I couldn't find solace in a lot of my passions for a long time.

After a whole year, I started restoring the energy and willingness, but the market and the rules on social media had changed by the time my heart, mind, and body were doing fine. At this time, especially during these last months, clout and likes play a major role and have the incredible capability to change your expectations. The number of micro-bloggers has escalated exponentially, expanding the chances to users from all over the world to create businesses and establish themselves as brands and online personalities. The global currency that is easily comprehended is fame, linked to numbers, likes, and views. But is this the goal, the means, or the way to gain fame? And what do you do once you have it?

Differently from other social media, Instagram is an image-based platform, where colors, hues, and aesthetic formats are essential to obtain an engaging delivery. In the fashion industry, Instagram has had its ups and downs. Started as an "instantaneous" application, Instagram's feeds in the early days were full of pictures taken with your own smartphone. There were pictures of sunsets, cake close-ups, or a sneak peek of the local bodega, but artistic effort was not the basis of the users. Between 2016 and 2017 Instagram began to be a global marketing tool, where analytics would play a huge role, and new jobs would be needed for brands and agencies. Influencers bloomed, numbers of followers, finstas, and start-ups became the trend and the standard.

Now, Instagram is facing a downturn, but at the same time it's being cautious in observing its members. Instagram communities rely a lot on images and videos, and the latter is what the social media app is aiming to be more and more creative on. IGTV, longer video uploads, and filters are all in the name of traffic and entertainment, and money that comes and goes among the creatives. As always, I can't speak for each and every one of the general public, but I can say that if you're on Instagram you probably share one universal goal: to stay in touch with a community, whether they are your real life friends, online friends, or coworkers. I can say that I've grown up with Instagram, at least since I was fifteen years old. Instagram has seen my presence on its platform for almost ten years, with different approaches and nicknames, from "gbaldini" to "giulisdreams," and ultimately, "thecurlyflower."

As an aspiring fashion journalist and college student, both Italian and Brazilian, living in NYC, I've realized that my contacts on social media are extremely diverse. In addition to that, my interests and the goals I want to achieve through my voice and writing go toward people who are social activists, politicians, and educators. I also allow myself to follow comedy pages too, since my creative writing is in constant need of humor and punchlines that can inspire and motivate me at the same time.

I won't lie, being recognized for your words, storytelling, and civic engagement in both the fashion and media industry would be an amazing and much-appreciated step to achieve. Regardless of the perks and the amenities I might be able to get from this status, I wouldn't want to be empty in my purpose and its ultimate goal. My dream to be a bridge among communities and speak up for the underrepresented is at the core of my mission. I see fame as an opportunity. I just want to channel and find these opportunities and turn them into something meaningful, for others and myself. How beautiful would it be to wake up every morning and do what you really want to do while being of service to the public in your own area of expertise? I aspire to be stuck in this comfort zone.

THE CURLY FLOWER AND FASHION ON THE BEAT

The story behind "the curly flower" is not known by a lot of people. "The curly flower" isn't even the nickname I was called in Italy. It came up in 2017 when I had to create a blog for one of my journalism classes, which turned out to be my professional blog, thecurlyflower.com. Since my early days on social media, my account names were either Giulia Baldini or giulisdreams. When I had to change my name for the blog, I decided to change it also for my other social media accounts, including Instagram, Tumblr, and Twitter. Behind this name there's a lot of symbolism. I chose the word "flower" because I wanted to honor my father, who's a botanist, researcher, and natural science professor. I used the adjective "curly" because I wanted to honor the only physical feature that I liked and was mostly talked about wherever I was, from Italy to the U.S.: my curly hair. I also wanted to give a subtle reference to my town, Florence, whose name means "the city of flowers." I've also been fond of flowers and nature since childhood, and my tropical side that I pulled from my mom kicked in when I was formulating my nickname.

I named my blog "the curly flower," but I decided to call this book Fashion on the Beat.

Fashion on the Beat is a multimedia project. It's a book, just like the one you've got right now in your hands, but it is also the name of this dream of mine that includes visuals, audio, words, and tangible in-person experiences. Its title comes from the fact that I see fashion as a song, an album, a collection of tracks. Fashion works just like music, with a series of fluid movements and shifts that keep you woke, relaxed, informed, and pumped. Fashion glows, shows, and flows. Fashion involves all the human senses and goes beyond the physics, through earthly materials and pragmatic needs.

As much I wanted to write a book that included instruction on how to make it in the fashion or journalism industries, I've realized that what we're living is an extremely fragile moment, full of unexpected dynamics and shifts. So, I decided to share my experience, knowledge, and thoughts. I created Fashion on the Beat to be a platform and a series of projects that can flow and sprout in the most vibrant and engaging industries. Just like how its founder, the curly flower, is watering her roots to grow and flourish wherever she wants to be. To stay tuned, make sure to check thecurlyflower.com for further updates, content, and much more that will come along the way.

FASHION JOURNALISM SHOULD HAVE ITS OWN BEAT

In my first semester of college, I realized how music has always been a passion of mine. It's been a long time since I have sung, and it's been a long time since I've felt comfortable singing too. Since I was never given the chance to fully express my artistic skills at home very openly, I've always tended to keep them low-key. However, since my arrival at college, I've discovered music with a different mindset and approach.

Music attracts me just like fashion because it's an industry that I've never thought I could have any serious interest in, but it saved me on many levels and helped me to craft my writing and language skills, especially in English. While listening to music, I found the existence of podcasts, and I started to listen to radio shows. I'd like to integrate my passion for music with my interest in fashion journalism, by explaining what it is, what its goals are, and what kind of lessons it can teach society.

There are three ways that I can transport fashion into an auditory experience:

1. Descriptive communication

Given the nature of fashion, the industry is made up of and works with thousands of visuals and fabrics. But how is it possible to describe what stylists, designers, and consumers experience with their eyes and the textiles they touch? If we develop a descriptive language among a broader community, people could more easily grasp the beauty of the products the fashion industry shows off. Basically, it'd be nice to say something is "beautiful" or "ugly" without using those words themselves, which are too vague and plain when it comes to fashion.

2. Talk and give voice to the members of the industry: models, stylists, art directors, makeup artists, etc.

Dedicating an audio platform to fashion journalism would provide a place for creatives to get noticed more and more. Their words and points of view would become more relevant and important, along with the messages and statements they plan to implement in their works. Often, artists struggle to get across what they would like to communicate. On the other hand, people have a hard time understanding the message behind a piece of clothing. This platform could be an instrument for creatives to make their message clearer and more approachable.

3. Conversational education

Being able to talk within a community opens a space where dialogues and points of view become the protagonists of a show. Conducting and following Instagram live sessions with these intentions would set the standard for an educative conversation, where people can learn and share thoughts and feelings.

As a flower, I aim to vividly blossom and turn into a marvelous life form that can live, learn, and possibly inspire others. My intention is to keep up with this positivity, explore how people find their daily dose of optimism, and see how wonderful life can be within small gestures, talks, and characteristics. And so that's me, my pen name, my personality, my total self: the curly flower.

CHAPTER 4

SUSTAINABLE FASHION AND TRENDY ISSUES

———

You're hurt the moment you don't talk
When you don't ask
When you don't speak up
When you don't show
something or nothing
You're loved the moment you write
When you give time to grab
a pen and a paper
the phone and your thumb
and write and type
and show
something or nothing
If I like you, you saw me hurt and loved
I showed you
something
and
nothing
tvb

WHAT'S IN VOGUE ISN'T IN VOGUE ANYMORE

The number of articles and social media posts I've read giving suggestions on how to deal with COVID-19 are countless. The internet is showcasing a powerful connection and solidarity in any field and within several communities. Just look at the #dontrushchallenge on TikTok. Creative women of all colors, sizes, and religions came together to represent different communities. The phenomenon is less superficial, though, and a lot more tangible for our wallets. Jobs and education are at risk. But solutions are being provided. Look at the #BlackLivesMatter (#BLM) movement along with the LGBTQ+ representation that the media is portraying more and more.

Being connected and finding support in your field has become the topic of many conversations. Since the beginning of quarantine, academics, social workers, performers, entrepreneurs, and media professionals have adapted their ethics and etiquette to a new workplace, now work space: online. The only bubble of society that is more present in the actual field is the science community, but even now its members are striving to find solutions through the media industry, the government, and the multimillion-dollar institutions that can financially help them.

What concerns me around the COVID-19 situation are the long-term results that the disease is creating among industries.

The fashion industry is adapting quickly to the current regulations. Some might suggest that fashion shows will go digital, others are speculating on webinars, social media presence, and streaming services. However, dealing with a seasonal market and a large audience of clients on a global scale will be an extreme challenge for the major fashion houses. Luxury houses will suffer less, given their strong branding strategies and versatility (since their investments are not solely relying on their clothing products). But small designers and creatives in the making are more vulnerable to falling behind, or even going bankrupt. Once again, the fashion hierarchy will be posh on its own terms and play a cruel game of selection.

Journalism appears to be in danger too. As I've always stated, being multifaceted and curious about your surroundings, both mentally and physically, are two of the best qualities both a professional and a creative could benefit from. Desperate times calls for desperate measures, and COVID-19 seems to be that occasion. Many journalists are dedicating time to shift their interests into tech, real estate, and other similar ventures. Marketing is also one of the top choices, as well as event management and social media positions.

No matter how many times I've heard it, being focused on just one or two interests will not give you as many opportunities as you would need. You have to expand your channels. Having a full plate is good to enjoy, but the fuller, the better. You will have more for you and for those around you. My behavior hasn't changed much since the beginning of quarantine because I've continued networking on my own and filling my passions with all the instruments I can afford. What has devastated me, mentally, is the ability to actually meet people in person. However, this is a universal feeling for the majority. I had made specific plans to attend events and complete bureaucratic procedures in the months of March, April, and May, very important ones for an international student (OPT application, apartment hunting, job and volunteering positions to look after). This is already complicated for an American citizen, but just imagine for an international student or immigrant, especially if they are here with no family, property, or without full financial independence. Still, I manage to recognize what I have and work with my strengths.

I tend to stay as connected and educated as possible among those who can provide me relevant news in the media and fashion industries. Now more than ever I am fully invested in politics, with which I have always had an on-again, off-again relationship. This last fact proves my privilege because my absence in knowing the exact current dynamics has slowed me down in the past, while learning other academic stuff. I had the luxury of going to school and being financially educated to manage my own savings, but I was never on top of the news like I am now. As somber as it might sound, this quarantine has been an opportunity to stay more virtually connected with topics I would tend usually give less attention to.

HOW MONEY COMES AND GOES IN THE FASHION INDUSTRY

New York Fashion Week 2020 in February was a bit different. Well, on a personal level it was pretty much the same as last year. But I was just remembering the first time I walked, and much has changed: my confidence, posture, interests, and mindset. I'm much more attentive and connected with the news, the industry, and the connections I have. My perspective changed as well. I've attended a couple of shows: one runaway, one opening party, and a showcase, plus I got the chance to walk in one show for African By

Art. However, as a fashion junkie with a hint of investigative and journalistic attitude, I couldn't ignore the news around fashion week, and how the whole business around it is drastically changing.

Articles and people claimed that fashion week is not a trending thing anymore. And I could see it. I realized that fashion week events, specifically New York Fashion Week, are becoming a whole series of multimedia events intertwined with fashion, but not only about fashion. What is trending in New York is the market and the fluidity that the industry is facing daily and every season. This is indeed the reflection of a city and society full of diversity. For this reason, a variety of performances and representation are demanded and expected in a center like the Big Apple.

I concluded that fashion is being more global and inclusive, as well as divided and somehow stagnant in their marketing mobility. There must be a change, and it is an inevitable one. This could be an aspect of the industry prone to change, but now this is what it looks like. And I'm not talking only about clothes, but also accessories and beauty products.

All these issues raise solutions and plans that are taking space in the market. Is it a solution to shift events like New York Fashion Week from a fashion manifestation to an assembly of fashion-related events in a massive way? Where is the future of fashion? I believe that it's going to be spread worldwide and without a center unless we're considering the economics. The center still looks to be between New York, London, and Milan. However, besides sustainability, are there any other plans that we should consider implementing in fashion?

Sustainability is a big theme now in fashion. Sustainability is a recurrent term in fashion, but what makes something sustainable? Who decides such a label? Who can use it?

In Los Angeles, I visited the Buffalo Exchange for the first time. I bought a dress with printed sunflowers. The following day, I walked down Melrose Avenue browsing every clothing store. While I was looking, I felt that this experience was fun, interesting, and at the same time good for my spirit. My ethical approach to fashion spiked to an unexpected level by getting more and more interested in sustainability. The feeling sparked again in Atlanta, where I visited vintage stores full of stylists, designers, and experts in the industry. The clothing at these resale clothing stores was more than art. The clothing was business, the stores were dealerships, the shopping was quality-searching and style-hunting, and all with the same objective: make a less negative impact on the planet while keeping the love for fashion alive. Buying or swapping clothes is indeed a good act for the planet since the fashion industry is one of the top three most polluting industries in the world. Plus, sustainable fashion connects more people and makes them appreciate their clothes more. The experience was art and communication together.

Amid leaving our campus during the first COVID-19 spread, I was left with tons of my friends' clothes and garment pieces. That made me think about our generation and how we should manage our wardrobes. We indeed need an education that enhances the importance of going green in our aesthetics. This will have huge impact on Earth and make our society a more conscious one.

College students are known to be broke, prone to buying the cheapest clothes on sale, and highly enthusiastic in following trendy brands. However, the first feature is the most universal one. Between the ages of seventeen and twenty-three, fashionistas live the struggle of the economic hustle, which includes balancing a career with a social life, by investing in their education and entrepreneurial businesses. According to a GoBankingRates.com study, the average American household spends around $1,860 purchasing clothes.[15] In other countries, like Italy, men tend to spend more on clothes than women.

When I visited Atlanta in 2019, I met Kenneth Christopher, a New Yorker, in Georgia. Kenny is a vintage apparel and record dealer. He curates his store, called "Little Five Vintage," in the neighborhood of Little Five Points. After visiting his store, I wanted to hear Kenny's thoughts on the fashion industry, thrift stores, and vintage clothing in critical times like these.

- How did you come across fashion, and why did you decide to work in this field?

My initial exposure to fashion was a high school retail job at a business that is no longer operating, American Apparel. Before I worked this job, fashion was just a generic thing to me, not something that made a person unique. Through this job I was exposed to a multitude of different styles, and eventually it sparked a real interest in fashion. I was able to

---

15   Grace Lin, "Are You Spending More Than the Average American on 25 Everyday Items?"

see how deeply it affected people, and that was something I desperately wanted to be part of.

- Can you describe your business?

The business I'm in is centered around vintage clothing, dating as far back as the 1920s. The majority of the vintage that I sell is comprised of original concert t-shirts, used military garments, and an array of collectibles such as promotional posters, comic books, and original records.

- What's the fashion scene in Atlanta?

The fashion scene in Atlanta is ever-changing. Atlanta is one of the meccas of African American businesses as well as a large entertainment industry presence. Because of this, fashion is incredibly important in the city. The large demand for fashion in Atlanta puts my business in a very unique position since we sell pieces that are incredibly hard to source and find. Since we offer a product that very few stores in the city are able to offer, we're able to control the market price of vintage in our area, whereas a business in another city, like Milwaukee for example, would be at the whim of their customers' needs. At my shop we mix modern with vintage in order to better help the customer transition from what they're normally used to.

- What's the future of vintage?

In the future vintage will become even harder to acquire and its market value will continue to increase because there is no way to reproduce authentic vintage. Pieces that aren't acquired by stores like mine sometimes end up destroyed or at city dumps, which means there is only a certain amount of vintage left in the world. Currently there are celebrities worldwide that are publicly photographed wearing vintage pieces, and when this happens the demand for it increases. In the future I see this trend continuing, and it will most likely make the vintage market more in demand over the years.

- How do you think this COVID-19 situation will impact your business?

The current coronavirus epidemic so far has increased my shop's business by almost 50 percent due to people not being able to attend school, and not having much to do during the day. Due to the economic decline because of the virus, this most likely will not last very long. I predict that the vintage industry will be in very real trouble until the virus is taken care of.

CIVIC ENGAGEMENT IN FASHION

Currently, I believe that my type of civic engagement has been mostly intimate and philosophical. I try to analyze matters of the heart and the issues related to fashion journalism with an op-ed tone. So far, my blog has been a mixture of everything. Some say a diary. Some say a journal. Others just say a collection of observations.

Knowing already what I want to focus on, I aim to craft my intentions and make them fit in the right situations, for the appropriate causes and specific goals. I just gotta sharpen my skills. There's always something to learn!

In a Euromonitor report done in 2017, the number of plastic bottles purchased per minute is equal to 1.3 million.[16] This is only one minor data among many that makes you think how much consumption practices influence our society and its behaviors. The numbers and other related facts about the state of our Earth, as well as the pollution caused by the fashion industry, led me to examine fast fashion.

Fast fashion is the type of marketing that happens in the fashion industry when a brand produces lots of products in a very short amount of time, with cheap fabrics and low budgets. The economy around fast fashion isn't safe nor does it provide any financial stability for the workers in it. The members of this industry who mostly pay high costs and put their lives in danger are men and women in/from developing-rising countries, such as China, Indonesia, Vietnam, India, Bangladesh, etc.

A scandal surrounding the brand Fashion Nova has revealed the sad and harsh realities fast fashion has caused in the last three years.[17] The Cut reporter Hannah Golden wrote how through an aggressive strategy of partnering with Instagram influencers to sell cheap, form-fitting clothing, Fashion Nova's sales grew by around 600 percent in 2017. The brand has 17 million followers on Instagram but owes over $3.8 million in back pay to hundreds of workers. And this is only one example of how fast fashion operates in the social media world, providing temporary pleasures to its clients and low salaries to its workers, who receive only $2.77 an hour.

---

16   @thevisioncom. Instagram post, February 19th
17   Hannah Gold, "Workers Making Fashion Nova Clothing Are Wildly Underpaid."

Fast fashion has made clothes more accessible to the general public. According to UNICEF, there are 260 million children in employment, with 170 million of the children working in the fast fashion industry.[18] Fast fashion is a side of the fashion industry where production, marketing, and labor operate at a fast pace with the main purpose of serving masses of clients at a reduced price. Many garments and accessories are produced in this way.

While I was researching potential sources for this book on sustainable fashion, I ended up watching a TED Talk video with Tamara Jones. Tamara had a speech at the TEDxRyersonU called "Life in the Slow Lane."[19] In this speech, Tamara illustrates her views and opinions on sustainable fashion. To this day, Tamara receives lots of messages thanking her for her honest speech, in which she shared relatable thoughts, questions, and concerns that the younger generations have at heart. I asked Tamara a couple more questions.

- How does sustainability in fashion play a role in your life? How did you come across the subject?

Sustainability plays a role in my overall consumption habits and the companies I choose to support. It has shifted my sense of style and aesthetic. I came across it during my time at school while learning about supply chains and environmental sociology, but I'd been thrifting clothing since high school.

---

18 Josephine Moulds, "Child labour in the fashion supply chain: where, why and what can be done?"

19 Tamara Jones, *Life in the Slow Lane*, video.

- As a journalist yourself, do you foresee any journalistic approach in fashion when it comes to sustainability? Think about transparency or ethics in the fashion field and how journalism could approach these issues in fashion itself.

I wouldn't call myself a journalist, more so a creative writer and culture writer. The difference is that I know that when I'm writing a creative piece it's inherently subjective, so there's always an agenda either explicitly or subconsciously. I'd love to see fashion journalism take on some of the ideas of business journalism: greenwashing investigations, uncovering supply chain inefficiencies, etc.

- Do you consider yourself an activist? Can you see nowadays social activism in fashion?

No, I don't. I consider myself more of a researcher than an activist. I honestly just like to learn about social issues, distill the information and share what I've learned with my community. I support the work of activists by donating and showing up at rallies, being engaged in the political process, but I wouldn't consider myself to move within that space as an activist.

- Is it possible to write about fashion, specifically sustainable fashion? What are the methods and techniques?

I think fashion journalists used to have their hands tied by a desire to have access to all these houses and companies and ad buys to keep publications alive. It might have been less of a payoff to expose unethical practices within their business models, but I think audiences are savvier now. It's up to journalists to point out the inadequacies and hypocrisies of the companies they cover for their audience. That's integral to the mandate of providing a fair and balanced perspective.

For example, with respect to some fast fashion CSR (corporate social responsibility) initiatives it's journalists' job to report on the existence and intention of the initiative, but also how the company falls short and whether the initiatives can realistically address the issues the company says they'd like to address. It's also up to fashion journalists to give people more options when it comes to sustainable fashion. It's not all about buying the latest ethically sourced denim or pineapple leather. It's about consuming less and reusing more. I'd love to see fashion writers highlight people who sew their own clothing, teaching people how to mend items and make them last, about fabric care, and less on trends and business reporting.

- I came across your work and profile through your TED Talk. How do you define that experience and what are the impacts you think you've made?

That was a surreal experience. I still get messages from people letting me know how much they learned from or enjoyed my talk. It's humbling. I actually applied to that on a whim in my last year of university to challenge my apprehension of public speaking, and I chose sustainable fashion because I was just genuinely interested in it at the time and making that transition myself. I was just immersed in it. There's already so much information about sustainability and fashion innovation in general out there, so I think my synthesizing the information and making it digestible, like pointing out tangible things we can do or stay conscious of as we go about our days, has had an impact. This information isn't new at all, I just pointed out a mental and behavioral shift that needs to take place if we want to create a more ethical marketplace.

A THOUGHT ON COMMUNITY SERVICE AND SOCIAL ACTIVISM

Western societies seem to have woken up and realized their privileges for the most part. With COVID-19 and the most recent protests against police brutality, donations and volunteering positions have risen up, but pragmatic solutions aren't that common. At least, that's what the media wants us to think. However, we can all agree that community service isn't a trend, but a lifestyle. Being a social activist makes you either a good person or a bad person. It depends on your approach and the agenda behind your interests. It wouldn't hurt to think that most of these social activists we're seeing online or on the streets are both good and bad community servers.

No matter how generous people are, I can't help but to be a bit skeptical. I wonder if the civic engagement that people are displaying is truly felt and perceived. Specifically, when it comes to Black Lives Matter, I can spot both a solid community made of people who want to move forward and instill changes, but I also see a lot of division among Blacks and Browns. Since George Floyd passed away on May 25th, the U.S. demanded change and the revolution started once and for all. A lot of police brutality cases came back again. Issues of colorism, blackface, cultural appropriation, and systemic racism have been discussed, but what are the solutions that we're fronting? Who is the we on the battlefield?

The people who are asking for justice are the ones who were born and grew up in the Black and Brown communities in the United States. African Americans and POC immigrants are the protagonists of these ongoing events, but their inner divisions carry a lot of weight on their progression and advocacy toward justice. Why is that? Some people think that looting is the solution. Others join social media challenges that are temporary, by enhancing the importance of old school organizations, publications, and other institutions. At the end of the day, it seems as though even Black people are still focused on entering the society they're in by attacking those institutions that have harmed them, instead of dismantling it with innovation.

What is the thing that American Black and Brown activists are really doing then? How can they really serve their communities? What can we all do?

To enter a fresh society with new laws and systems, it is necessary to be educated and know what our position is in all these events. We must recognize our differences first and foremost. White people need to learn to listen, Black people need to speak up with a cohesive voice. Biracial people need to validate their whiteness and Blackness, get rid of any damaging social passes they benefited from, and be informative for their counterparts. Other POC and non-white people need to understand that these are intersectional issues that touch them too, no matter what their background is or where they are currently located. Being a POC is a universal experience, so this should matter to all of us POC around the world. The world is becoming less impregnated with white supremacy because non-white realities are blossoming and becoming the new realities. However, white supremacy is still real, and we really need to be engaged in social activism. But how? What are we doing bad or wrong, and good or right?

We need to be careful about what we're paying attention to and what causes we're supporting. Community service and social activism are at the core of civic engagement. It goes beyond mere performance in the streets, with a grunge attitude and an urban pride. It isn't a pure and ethereal collection of acts that will solve all the problems, but rather as a tool to organizing power within a society, on a political, moral, and ethical manner.

Dear POC. Dear Black and Brown people. Haven't you noticed how many media organizations and companies have apologized to us for their behaviors? Isn't it weird that they needed so many tragedies and complications to realize how wrong and racist they have been for so long? How much cultural appropriation and loitering have they been doing? They think that turning their PR departments and Media Advisory members into small social activist agencies will dissolve their wrongs. Will their behavior change, though, once this wave of social activism ends? How long will this cycle last? Is it normal at all, or should we focus on bringing and sticking to another form of normalcy? How damaging is this approach to community service and social activism? Do you feel the need to help me because you see my struggles and you want to feel good about yourself?

As a recent graduate willing to enter the media industry, these times are extremely remarkable. Every bit of information and series of events I am witnessing are part of my very first chapter of adulthood. I am grateful for having completed my academic journey, which has lasted more than ten years—from my Florentine days to the American ones in college. Now I feel like I can put in motion what I've learned in the books. At the moment I can't afford to donate or go to all the protests I'd like to go to, engage in every single activity that I would like to support with my physical presence, but I can use my smartphone and my laptop keyboard to release my stream of consciousnesses and report the events I'm living. Through my writing and reading, I can also get access to educative resources that can teach me how to sharpen my communication skills.

CHAPTER 5

INVEST IN YOUR CREATIVITY

———

Respect my love. Respect my hurt feelings.
Respect my traumas. Respect my peace.
Respect my respect toward you. Respect my friendship.
Respect my passions. Respect my accomplishments.
Respect my independence. Respect my freedom.
Respect my culture. Respect my past. Respect me.
-what I want for my birthday, and I'm born every day

If you know me or have had the chance to have me as your roommate, between assignments, my daily writing, and my weekly fitness exercises, I enjoy watching cartoons, TV series, and documentaries. This has to do a lot with my first and foremost passion, the reason why I came here to NY: screenwriting.

Even though in four years my interests grew deeper in other areas (fashion modeling) and shifted to other forms of writing and expression (journalism and poetry), my habit of imagining and reporting stories through visuals never ceased.

However, no matter how much I enjoy drawing curly dolls with big eyes in my journals, I never thought I had a knack for sketching on a professional level. But I've always appreciated art. In fact, it was because of my appreciation that I got my very first modeling gig in New York. The rest is all history and a journey on its way.

Due to the times we're all experiencing with COVID-19, I know that creatives are struggling. I talk a lot about how to invest your creativity with all the means you can get and afford. I don't have a lot of capital, but I have a clear vision of what I want to accomplish. I want to represent the underrepresented, be a bridge between the communities I am involved in and be a cosmopolitan individual. For this reason, I've decided to allocate some space on my blog and Instagram feed to connect with illustrators and digital artists, who are willing to collaborate with me to bring up colors and style under and in front of my eyes.

Working in the media industry as content creators or reporters always makes you think about the stuff that you write, post, share, and execute, and ultimately question its worth. Creatives are in the same boat, including models, actors, and creative writers.

If you work in a company, you might have found yourself in the position of wondering if you can ride solo or with a friend of yours and start your own thing. If you already work alone, you want to step up your game and make your art valuable. However, how can you benefit from being creative in a world whose immediate needs aren't related to your field? Do you feel guilty about obsessing over these thoughts of yours, legitimate and ambitious, but also almost selfish and driven toward an obscure goal?

Who doesn't want to make money out of what they most like to do? I had the luck to grasp the most energetic vibes among different groups of creatives in the fashion and media scene in New York, LA, and Atlanta. I could showcase to them my enthusiasm, I could see a profit coming from my passion (projects, collaborations, deals), and a reciprocate interest from these people. For this reason, I plan to sharpen my obsession to invest in my creativity while writing.

Discipline is required to set both an intellectual and a pragmatical structure to play by. Getting an education gives you the chance to enhance your knowledge, and it doesn't need to be academic. Multiple online or on site resources can help you to learn a new skill that can become useful in your business. Lastly, being patient is key to give yourself time and recognition for what you're doing. Being patient is one of the most difficult parts in expanding my creativity. Whenever I release either a journalistic article or a creative writing piece, or a photoshoot or a podcast episode I helped produce, I wonder if what I did was relevant or if I will ever be comforting someone's heart. To master all this, a long journey must be taken.

You reach an age when you think how money is made, and if you're child, you probably want to just buy a printer and print the bills. But they tell you that actually you can't do this. At least, that's what they told me. This was back in the early 2000s. Currencies now are digital, the market is becoming more and more paperless, and the ways to earn money have exponentially grown.

Being an entrepreneur isn't for everyone. These days, the term "entrepreneur" is used loosely, almost as a replacement of "businessman" or "businesswoman." Entrepreneurship is admirable, but it comes from a sufficient desire to make an income from nothing. Unfortunately, not everyone has the skills, the interest, or the patience to embark on this path.

Sometimes I do see myself as an entrepreneur because I have a set of ideas that I cannot wait to put out. However, I must recognize that to become an entrepreneur, I must have and show a talent. My personal talent is writing—the product I ultimately plan to sell and market myself with—and building bridges among communities, within the media industry, specifically the fashion, the editorial, and the movie industry (screenwriting). I see myself making money from my writing and my other media ventures: podcasts, TV shows, art galleries, liberal arts school programs, etc.

As you might know, I am a firm believer in engaging with your community. The contacts you make and the people you consider friends and dear ones have the powerful capacity to influence your actions and thoughts.

If I'd need to choose a term to describe my financial choices, I would use the word "minimal." Being minimalistic in your expenses has been a trait of mine since the beginning of college, primarily due to two factors: not being able to earn an income as an international student (except for a few jobs on campus) and being a minimal fashionista (sticking to a selective wardrobe has cut my budget). However, I found other ways to be educated around money:

- Surround yourself with people who know about this topic.

- Choose friends who make good decisions for themselves, who are emotionally healthy and willing to be present in your life.

- Take courses that can help you investing in yourself. I found so many free conferences, seminars, and online resources through Instagram, Facebook, and Twitter.

Even though I understand the presence of these incumbent thoughts, the fear of rejection or not being treated as an equal are right in front of me. In addition to these feelings, normal in a senior college student, the pandemic we're living in doesn't make things easier. Employment seems scarce and extremely difficult to achieve.

One thing that I've noticed while applying for jobs or just talking with journalists and professionals in the fashion industry is that a restricted number of recruiters are open to talking with international students or are even aware of different kinds of visa documentation. If you're an international student and you're reading this, I will tell you this right away: no matter what field you are in or plan to be, the paths you'll take will always differ from the ones you have been taught at regular academic workshops or networking events. This aspect is comprehensible. But many times, I felt frustrated because I had to make three or four times the effort to explain my situation in an elevator pitch, highlighting my interests as a creative and professional. Sometimes I still feel that way, I can't lie. However, I have taken time to understand my rights and capabilities, and to practice my pitches and networking skills.

In addition to doing my own work, I've also learned to listen to others and skim through the myriad of contacts I've collected since the very beginning of college. Now it is time to get my voice out, more than ever, as well as to lend my ears to the most valuable voices.

Again, I do feel discouraged sometimes because I'm still in a position where I have to reach out to thousands of people in order to get only three or four answers. I try to not take anything personally, but I recognize and live through the confusion and pain. It's exhausting. I'm so confident in my message and personality, but as a human being, I fear not being considered or even muted. I do have a voice and I will keep offering my time and knowledge to represent the under-represented among different communities.

MOTIVATION

Intention is key to consistency. Motivation happens when there's a specific willingness to act and do something about your existence, which in my case is to write to represent the underrepresented. I always stress the importance of my intention because this is the main way I keep myself motivated. The fashion industry is such a fast business, in addition to the editorial world. In both, everything is frenzied, and it is hard to keep up with what's new and useful. Nevertheless, this is the job of a true fashionista, a fashion aficionado, and as a fashion journalist.

Pumping myself up with positive motivation is the only way I'm able to create a safe environment for myself and my passions. Everything is balanced and clear when I know what my purpose is and how I can be of service to society. My words carry a different weight if I put trust in them. To trust in my own words, I have to stick with my ideas and values, whose meanings and goals are meant to be heard. At the end of the day, human beings are social animals that require compassion, understanding, and a collective existence within a community. They do need to be loved. For me, love is in fashion, the interactions I have, and journalism. Just like in everything that you do and imagine, reality is the result of an idea's execution. Pursuing a dream is a doable action that requires consistency. In order to have consistency, motivation must be set as the basis of every one of your thoughts.

One day when I was in Italy, one of my dearest friends and I went out to get a cup of coffee. It was a cold and gray Florentine morning, but nothing stopped us meeting in one of the most elegant coffee places in the city. We chatted a bit, and then she told me something. She confessed to me how much she admires me, how strong I am, and what a woman I have become. I was a bit confused because I was the one who always admired her, and I wasn't expecting the opposite at all. Back in the day, she was the fiercest one in front of me, full of life, attention, and romance. But apparently, I've always made this positive impression on her, despite my being the nice and cute friend who was not liked by any boys at school and too geeky to go out on a Saturday night.

I was a role model to her. A bit unexpected, but this was not the first time someone or a friend of mine said that I inspire them. I've always been known as the outsider, a sweetie, a good girl. The one who puts love first, no matter what. The "weak," some might say. The one who gets her heart broken or ignored. My friend's comment this time caught me by surprise because I'm currently living a fragile moment. All I could think was: "How do I keep my positivity up? How did I become this positive? How am I being positive? Am I good? Damn it, I'm living in hell! How?"

It is true indeed that in four college years, I have developed a new set of behaviors and attitudes that drastically changed my view of life. I have built a shell to protect myself from the negative things around me. I did that through travel, meditation, and academic focus. For a long time, all I wanted was to change because I wanted some form of approval. I wanted to be seen as a girl. Now I want to be seen as a Brown young woman, whose skin color and body features can take space and tell a story. Once I figured out what I clearly wanted for myself, and what kind of position I wanted in society, there was a moment when I was tired of being sad. So, I ceased all the unnecessary worries and started living day by day.

For this reason, my so-called positivity and joie de vivre have grown. I started caring less and less about the people who didn't reciprocate my affection and interest, in every single aspect of my life. I demanded only to walk myself into spaces and situations where I would feel welcomed and appreciated, where I could be seen for exactly who I was in the flesh. I began doing what I like most, which meant traveling, writing, and talking about fashion within a listening community.

I tried to incorporate all my academic knowledge into my hobbies and connect everything with anything that would cross my mind. I found myself lonely, but never alone. Often, I felt alone and going against my peers' trends, but I kept sticking to what I believed in as well as listening to whoever was around me. And that's how I somehow irradiated my light that I thought was lost forever.

I recognized that my positive attitude resided in the fact that I was comfortable on my own, trusted solely myself, and stopped comparing myself to others. They are they. I am not them. That can't change. Move on. Be in your body. You're in control of it, so do it. I did it. Inside, I changed. Beautiful. Social media has helped me find positive accounts, from which I learn and find my balance through their words every day.

Music is another medium I use to develop and keep up my self-love. Sometimes silence is much needed because you just need to be in your own thoughts, in your own body with no words floating around or inside your ears. But songs are life and they do keep you inspired. As a polyglot and communications student, on several occasions, music was the only bridge I could use to grasp the essence and nature of my surroundings.

I believe that conversations and inspirations between women are significant and have a more solid weight. Feminine support is much needed and fundamental, especially in your twenties. We all live with struggles, but we also shine each other's lights. I firmly believe in that. The table must be kept small, but we can have tons of food to eat and share with each other. Motivation has come from this source too, because it is refreshing to witness the growth of your friends as models, artists, and entrepreneurs. Even as a college student, at the end of the journey you can see what has outgrown or solidified between you and your dear colleagues.

I do need my own time and space. At this particular time of my life, I always feel the need to isolate myself. But my passion for journalism and fashion, along with my bursting creativity, push me constantly to get out of my stagnant zone. I'm aware that my positivity is real because it has its ups and downs, but I know that I can always seek a solution. Nothing is still in life. At first, I was uncomfortable with this fact, but once I started accepting it, my mindset became more relaxed and apt to work under much more pressure. In fashion everything comes and goes. There are praises and backlashes every two seconds. But if there's a collective intention you can see yourself into, that will become your love and an intrinsic part of you. The only thing you can't escape is death. The rest shall be lived. It's worth it. I say this because I once thought that ending life was the solution. No, it's not. And what saved me was fashion, writing, and a world of color, life!

I've been spending my senior year winter break at home, differently from the previous break, which I spent in Brazil. Both these last two trips to my motherlands have been informative and constructive. They made me see my own countries with nostalgic eyes, an outsider mindset, and a personal affection for them. I went to Italy with a warm heart and a fervent mind, ready and willing to absorb as much information as possible, especially about my origins, family, friends, and purely myself. Given this attitude, I started taking my writing more seriously and giving myself much more credit. I'm at a point in my life where everything is unsure, I'm very much alone in my choices, and I'm forging my thoughts and feelings solely by myself—as it should be. My motivation is moved also by a necessity of representation. I write, in fact, to represent the underrepresented, specifically young Brown girls.

REPRESENTATION

In her TED Talk called "The Danger of a Single Story" Chimamanda Ngozi Adichie reveals the experiences she had to go through as a writer and young Black woman to find and shape her voice. The Nigerian-born writer says how important is to consider stereotypes as not the general truth, but only as a general depiction and representation of a society.22 This made me think of myself, as my identity is not fully Italian or Caucasian or Brazilian. The earliest days I can remember, I always had the tendency to write stories that had the same pattern of Tom Sawyer, Huckleberry Finn, and Little Women. I still have memories of writing like I was Becky Thatcher, a girl who was liked by Tom Sawyer and had incredible adventures with him. I never considered the very deep nature of these books, or the historical context, even though I knew that they were written in the nineteenth century. But I never questioned the possibility that actually other narratives could be shaped and remade, without losing the dreamy atmosphere that stories with the same types of characters—mostly white, blonde, and with blue eyes—portrayed.

For this reason, I needed to find a way to act and speak up for myself. I couldn't bear the silence anymore, the stillness in my life, or the self-pity I was suffocating in. In my subconscious I was seeking different stories and people with something to say, to live for, to stand for. If I couldn't hear these narratives, then I would look for them. And that's what I did, and how I found my spot in fashion journalism.

I mostly write in English for an English-speaking audience, but I've realized that there's a huge, more urgent than expected, need of diverse representation in Italy, especially in journalism. I already knew this fact, since Italy is a predominantly white country led mostly by old, elitist men. No matter how beautiful and charming Italians are, our political and sociological systems are old and sometimes outdated. However, with the eyes of a journalist, I've seen activism and had constructive dialogues, both from people of the left and right wings. I've met people who are willing to learn more, and others who are comfortable in their small bubble. I took all these observations as a reminder to myself to keep doing my stuff and be more intentional, specific, and constant.

Once and for all, I felt how tangible the problems are that Italy and Italians are facing, which are rhetoric and representation. Italians know how to talk, but they don't know how to listen and build constructive bridges, yet. Populism weights more than anything in our everyday life. Populism seems to be the only technique Italians use to deal with things. There's toleration, but not acceptance. More than half of Italians think that racist acts are acceptable.[20] Whether the political party is right or left wing, the representation of Black Italians

---

20 Angela Giuffrida, "More than half of Italians in poll say racist acts are justifiable."

in offices is extremely low, not even covering 25 percent of the total. There are Black and Brown Italians, as well as other biracial and mixed Italians. And yet, not enough representation. I don't see the same unity and pride that African Americans share among each other when it comes to Black or Brown Italians. How long will this situation be static? This is a general observation, though. Not everyone is like this, but the majority, no matter how liberal, democratic, or conservative they are, face this problem. Only Italians can fix this issue if they want to. And I hope they do.

As a biracial millennial, born and raised in Italy, with a mom of African-Brazilian heritage, the only moment where I would hear and learn about slavery or racial issues was with my aunts and uncles in Rio de Janeiro, Brazil. I was never given the tools and the information about that piece of history in any of the schools I've attended. I was lucky enough to be educated by my family on this issue, in addition to having a Caucasian father who is open to such conversations. I had to instruct myself around the topic of race, especially when asked who I was. I had many difficulties in adapting to American society. It wasn't a linguistic barrier, but mostly a cultural one.

Coming from Europe, you'd see America as this white country that TV portrays, where Blackness is almost a synonym for gangs and violence, and white is seen as pure and patriotic. Given my appearance, I look Hispanic or even like a biracial African American. Being a fashion model in New York has been a challenge because castings require you to select a race or they ask you what your heritage is. At first, I didn't know what to say. They started to assume

I was just Black or Latina. I had to do my readings and have conversations with my female friends to understand who I was in a society that I was welcomed into, while at the same time looked down or judged in. Nowadays, I identify myself as Brown, biracial, Italian-Brazilian, or Afro-Latina (considering Italy is a Latin country just like Spain and Portugal).

ACTION AND CREATION

Action occurs when the intention previously set is anchored in our mindset. What we want to achieve dictates how we communicate with whomever is around us. Through action I can access creation. While creating a concept I am able to analyze myself. I do an active check on myself. Fashion was able to cure my biggest insecurities and lift me up. Journalism gave me the right discipline with which I could abide in society, without feeling inadequate or out of context.

I have found struggles in my writing too. As a creative writer, I've wondered how to best address my stories to such a diverse audience consisting of so many different cultural backgrounds. Journalism saved and instructed me because it gave me the discipline and the structures to know more on how to use my words, how to make it prolific, concise, direct, and full of purpose. For this reason, I want to write to represent the underrepresented, and fashion journalism gives me the ability to perform my writing and creative skills at the same time.

I take action with whatever I have in my hands and on my mind. With my phone I use social media and my blog. Podcasts are great way to learn. Listening to podcasts has officially been a hobby of mine for almost two years. Podcasts are a significant, but still underrepresented, form of media, where any type of information can be discussed, such as: lifestyle topics, politics, medicine, religion, and so on. When it comes to podcasts, you only need one thing to follow a podcast episode, and that is a good ear. Listening is a skill that must be continually improved. Listening is not easy. Most of the time, especially in first world countries, hearing is what people do. You can hear a song and find it catchy, but not actually pay attention to the lyrics. You can hear someone's story, but you may not grasp the life lesson behind it. For this reason, podcasts are a form of communication that not everyone is willing to consider. To follow podcasts, you should be listening to the actual words that the people ask, tell, and discuss. Otherwise, it's just a waste of time.

Since my first year at Hofstra University, campus life has been a reality in my daily existence. I depend a lot on my academic calendar. As a college student, my finances are not always at their best. However, as a fashion lover and creative multimedia journalist, I'm always looking forward to great and vibrant events in the city. As some of you already know, my college experience has been a very peculiar one, and I've always tried to take the best from both my campus and urban experiences in NYC, and in the fashion industry. I genuinely love meeting new people because I believe that everyone is a storyteller in their own way, and I can learn from them, 24/7. So where do I meet people and listen to people's stories? Where do I find the sources for my blog, my ideas, and my writing?

Real talk: you don't meet new people, with good vibes, with your same exact interests, casually in the streets of

Manhattan. No. I mean, it's NYC, so, you can be blessed with such a marvelous encounter. But most of the time, if you want to go out, meet new people, and feel less intimidated by the new town/industry/place, then you have to push yourself out and attend events. Your phone's technology helps a lot too. I have found great tools via apps and online programs. Keeping up with the news in fashion is not impossible, and neither is gathering or publishing your own. You just need a solid group of sources that can facilitate your searches and make your education full of diversity and perspectives.

Start-ups are a great way to build and find a community around the fashion industry, because they are just starting and making progress just like you. Start-ups are more willing to listen and interact with you.

You must pay attention, especially in fashion more than journalism, to how you use and present your social media. It is not a matter of popularity or likes and following, as many would argue. Those elements are a huge help when it comes to marketing and advertisement. The core of making a good impression and the most efficient use that you can have with your social media handles is to follow and be followed by a respectable audience. The people you interact with should be the representation of who you are and what you intend to be. This is the way you show people who you are and what you can offer them.

Building a solid community on my Twitter and Instagram accounts has been beneficial and a major plot twist in my career as a freelancer, creative, and college student. The tools

I was given, including my blog, allowed me to keep up with the creative scene not only in New York, but also Los Angeles, Atlanta, and other cities in Italy and Brazil. In three full years, my connections in New York have seen some ups and downs because not everyone that you meet is going to be forever nice to you, and sometimes boundaries are necessary. However, most of the people I got to know in the editorial and fashion world have inspired me, grown along with me, and most importantly believed in me.

So, what do I actually do to find these souls in these crazy, colorful, gigantic industries?

- *I am myself all the time*, no matter who I have in front of me.

- I *don't sugar coat or exaggerate* anything regarding my work. What I've done is out there. And what I've not completed is in process, but there is no shame in saying "I'm working on X project," rather than selling it as already done. People can see your *honesty and professionalism* at the same time.

- I create my pitch. *I'm a business*. I treat myself like one. As a *writer*, I ponder and give meaning to every single word I use. As a *model*, I show my mindset. As a *creative*, I share my interests in a passionate and detailed way. I know my details, you can fact-check whatever I say.

- I dress *within my comfort*, never to impress. Plot twist: I'll impress people by showing them how comfortable I am in my clothes.

- I'm *more a listener than a speaker*. Probably because it's the innate nature of a polyglot, to actually enjoy listening to others. But I also like listening because it gives me more time to shape my narrative. After a verbal exchange I can offer a piece of information that the other might be into. I can serve them. In other words, I listen because I want to show *my respect to whomever I have in front of me*.

- I let the conversations *flow*. In a span of five minutes I can go from one subject to another and reconnect everything to what I initially said. I *never lose track* of what I'm saying.

- I'm honest. If I space out, I politely ask them to *repeat themselves*. Putting a silent mode on your ears is sometimes human nature, especially in crowded spaces. If the conversation turns out dull, I find ways to get myself out of that situation. It happens and it's *nobody's fault*.

- Make *eye-contact*. Coming from a Latin culture, I tend to kiss on the cheeks or hug a person when I first meet them. In the U.S. sometimes this is not the best way to approach people. I've learned this, but I also now know when and where I can be more Italian than in other scenarios. It's just a matter of *being present in the moment* and realizing what and what not to do.

I wasn't born with these manners. *I made them my own.* I had to engage connections with people and attend many workshops, fashion shows, cyphers, concerts, and networking events to understand how to move in this world, and in journalism and fashion.

IF YOU'RE A CREATIVE, THEN THIS IS FOR YOU!

I love reading and I'm an avid reader, but I'm also a slow reader. I like to take time while enjoying my books. Depending on what moment of my life I'm living, I find reading the most suitable and easiest therapy, and an economical one too. Reading You Are Here: Discovering the Magic of the Present Moment by Vietnamese Thich Nhat Hanh has been beneficial, and I'd love to share with you how this book has been good for me.[21] This could be useful to creatives too, who are sometimes in the loop of the "fear of missing out" (FOMO) lifestyle.

As a Zen monk, Thich Nhat Hanh teaches the importance of being alive and mindful in the present time. I decided to read this book because I wanted to know more about Buddhism. I have a great friend who is Buddhist, and I wanted to know more about her culture. She is very private and doesn't share a lot of details when it comes to her religion. In order to understand her more, I took the effort to read a book based on Buddhist lessons that could both help me understand my friend's culture as well as sharpen my meditation methods, which include silence and listening. The book is mostly about self-love and self-growth, but I tried to read between the lines and tried to also see how some of these words could actually be useful in my own life as a fashion journalist.

ON JOURNALISM

Journalism is fast and dynamic, but at the same time it has to be taken slowly and with the right mindset. There are actually

---

21   Thich Nhat Hanh, *You Are Here: Discovering the Magic of the Present Moment.*

no rights or wrongs in journalism, unless it's about ethics and transparency, which must be practiced under any circumstances by journalists. Considering all the facts and the data given around a specific situation is important to avoid making assumptions. Assumptions are false perceptions most of the time. Sometimes we make external situations personal and we suffer because of them. We don't need to do that. Taking a step back is good. Take time to analyze, write, speak up, and show up only once you have all the material with you.

All journalists are privileged to be in an industry where writing and expressing their opinions are requirements and aspirations. Not many people, like some journalists coming from places other than the United States, are able to access this privilege. Journalism has a lot of rules when it comes to writing and dealing with clients, corporations, agencies, and editors. However, this is a job that allows you to exercise your writing and your use of words. Getting paid for typing words that can shape a nation, a generation, or someone's mind is great, isn't it?

ON FASHION

Tons of errors have been made in the past. Blackface, gender-elitism, and lack of body positivity are just some of the things that have happened in the history of fashion. Some of us are ready to change this. We must acknowledge what went wrong and change it, now. Going back and fixing the past is not possible. We must be in the present, study the past, and learn from it. We can only fix the past by being present and mindful in the present. I think that this attitude should be more and more adopted in the fashion industry.

ON MENTAL HEALTH

I can't stress enough how essential taking care of yourself and your love language is. This note goes for your love life, but also for your external relationships. You are by nature always present for yourself, but you must be present and willing to give ears to others too.

As a college student, I've been through a lot in terms of getting to know myself and understanding my needs. I'm so glad to have many moments just for myself because that's the only way I can go to my friends with a better disposition. I can listen to them, be there for them, and take care of myself. I experienced a lot of mental solitude my last two years of college. I'm glad I've gone through that, no matter how much I cried and endured in pain. As much as I wanted to be close to some people or include them in my life, I realized that it wasn't actually my fault to be hungry for more mental, emotional, and solid support. When you focus on self-love you automatically raise your own bar in endless ways. And eventually you'll attract the people you both need and manifest their company.

In addition to my personal life, the words in You Are Here showed me how much I should be present in journalism and fashion. Due to their fast and rough intensity, there have been times when I wasn't able to keep up with the news in fashion or channel all my interests at once with the right instruments or information. It took time for me to understand how to do it, and I'm still on a journey. I want to master my curiosity and transparency among my passions, but I need to sharpen my skills more and more. One of these skills is to be present, and actively engage with both my peers and my mentors. This is the only way I learn, build my community, and grow a solid personality.

I hope you guys will read You Are Here by Thich Nhat Hanh. It's very enlightening. It will help you heal, be a better individual, and a person full of compassion, no matter what you're going through.

CREATIVITY IN THE FASHION INDUSTRY: JEFFREY BEANE FROM GREENSBORO, NORTH CAROLINA

I met Jeffrey at an open mic/cypher night in Brooklyn in the summer of 2019. My friend and roommate Victoria hosted the event, and I was there as a supporter, photographer, and friend. Yes, I can proudly say I'm naturally good at those three jobs. Jeffrey's performance caught my attention, and when he went off the stage, I showed my support by congratulating him and following his music page on Instagram. From that evening to now, we have mostly stayed in touch through social media. I like his music, but what I like more about him is his stage presence and delivery of his lyrics. I asked Jeffrey a few questions about his background, his story with the fashion industry, and his relationship with music. Jeffrey is not the only fashion talent who invested his energy in the music realm, but he was also one of the few whose charisma struck me. Dear readers, here we are with professional model and music producer/artist/songwriter Jeffrey Beane, a.k.a. E-Mars.

- Is there a particular moment or anecdote that made you realize that modeling was important to you?

It's kind of funny how I got into modeling, actually. It was my senior year of high school, and I was at school early preparing for jazz band and my teacher said, "I don't normally ask students this, but have you ever considered modeling?"

And my honest response was "No, not at all actually." So, he put me in contact with someone he knew in town. That ended up going nowhere, but it sparked my intrigue in the business. Around two years later I worked at Banana Republic, and my coworker was a model and stylist at a local agency, and he recommended that I email them. So long story short, I did, I met with them, and they signed me on the spot.

- What are the challenges of being a male model? Are there any stereotypes or stigmas around the job?

There are plenty of challenges to being a male model, both physically and emotionally. Especially since it's mostly a women's industry. I feel like as the world changes, the industry changes along with it. I almost felt like as a straight, white male, it is almost harder to book jobs, specifically in NYC, because that demographic was overplayed early on—like the early 2000s. That is how I feel, and what I have noticed from my personal experience. Since everyone is trying to be so diverse, they are almost coming full circle to exclusion again. It's oddly interesting.

- How would you make the industry more diverse and dynamic?

I would say the industry is more than diverse now. It's definitely come a long way and changed a lot over the past ten years alone. I think the industry is extraordinarily confusing. And most brands don't even know what they want until the last possible minute. Most of the people I have met are very nice and professional, but in terms of payment, I feel like six to eight weeks to receive a check is absurd.

- What do you do with music? What do you see in music that you don't see in modeling?

I have been into music since a very young age. I took piano lessons in elementary school, and I played clarinet for seven years through middle school and high school. Then in sophomore year of college, I picked up software music production on my own in the form of GarageBand, and I never looked back. I am mostly a self-proclaimed rapper. Rap is my main genre of interest. However, I try to be as versatile as possible to accommodate other artists. So, I make beats in the genres of pop and R&B as well as electronic dance music. And I see so much in music that I don't see in modeling, the main thing being freedom. Complete freedom of expression and ideas. I don't have to wait on other people to do their job because I have complete control. It is a euphoric feeling to be able to make something that provides joy and good vibes for myself and to be able to share it with others. I love music, both listening and creating it.

- Do you see any link between music and fashion as forms of art and types of industries?

There are plenty of parallels between music and modeling. They both take confidence and not giving a damn of the opinions of haters, they both take a lot of creativity and a lot of individuality as well as putting your personal spin on it in terms of ideas. They both require you to have to be able to be told "no" and continue moving forward without doubting yourself too.

- Why did you choose music as your passion to dig in?

I didn't choose music as my passion, music chose me. And as corny as that sounds, it's true. I literally never go anywhere without listening to music. It makes me happy and keeps me motivated in every aspect of my life. I am grateful for music because when I didn't have any friends, music was my friend. Hopefully, that doesn't sound that depressing, but it's true. Music makes you feel things, it makes you think and question how your life compares to other people before you. And music is infinite. It will always be there, and there are so many possibilities to explore it sonically.

GRADUATED CREATIVE ON THE BEAT

Coming to an end of this era, as an undergraduate college student, I'm entering a new phase, inside which I'm collecting every brick to build my career. The space I'm allocating myself has been mostly made of emotional support so far. In order to discover my own self and my passions, I needed to be surrounded by multiple people. Some of those people directed me further than others, some were just temporary lessons, others were difficult to deal with, others brought me pain and struggles, but all of them were fundamental in making me channel my feelings, personality, and work in the right places and with the most authentic effort.

I went through rough times and survived them because of my friends. I am thankful to have expanded and built this emotional immune system because living in New York City as an international young Brown woman into fashion and journalism—two tough industries—can be difficult and draining. There have been times when I wanted to give up everything. Sometimes I still think that what I want to do is impossible or too big for me, but my few good people are there to support me. They won't provide me solutions. They might not know how to navigate certain aspects of my interests as a model, writer, and immigrant. However, I know that they are willing to listen to me, no matter how far away or how long it takes them to text me back.

I now understand my passions more and what I want to get out of them. No matter what I want to do and what life will offer me, writing will be at the core of my passions. Through my writing, I hope to represent those whose voices are not loud enough, and with the colorful world of fashion I want to portray them and make them represented. I think that this is the kind of love that I should aim for because it's something that I enjoy doing and that people appreciate from me the most. Now that I know what I want to say and the people I'm surrounded by, I intend to upgrade and get into a new journey, the one where I get to be heard and seen through my words.

CHAPTER 6

THE VISUALS

Dear readers,

Being trilingual isn't an easy journey or lifestyle to stick with. Every day is a challenge to keep up with, but it gives you endless opportunities to connect with a multitude of people. When you get the chance to speak and read another language other than your native language, you mold another voice in yourself. Whenever I speak in Italian, my voice sounds different. From my perspective, I believe I have a firmer and more adult tone. When it comes to Portuguese, even though I am fluent, I can feel some Italian accent in my words. And yes, my Brazilian friends and family members don't miss an occasion to notice that. I learned not to take it personally and be a bigger person, embracing my accent in any shape and form. My Italian accent will naturally be prevalent in any language and idioms I speak because Italian is my first and foremost language. I learned it at home, in school, and with friends and most of my acquaintances since birth. However, I recognize the privileges that come with being a polyglot, and for that I will always be grateful for my parents, especially my mom, Mamãe.

I had several conversations with both my Italian and American friends regarding the best and most efficient ways to learn and practice a second or third language. My process has always relied on verbal and written communication with mainly three channels of apprenticeship: music, books, and movies. The power of written words accompanied by vocals and visuals has a tremendous impact on an individual's psyche.

When they say that books are important to read, I completely agree with that. I can affirm that reading books is imperative for learning anything, from mathematics to natural sciences, from interior designing to sustainability in fashion.

However, I recognize that reading is not one of the most tempting things to do. I have a great portion of friends who don't consider reading one of their top activities or even part of their favorite hobbies.

In the past, I would be discouraged to talk about my readings or just my reading interests with them, simply because I thought I would sound boring and bring only annoying vibes to the table. In college, especially during my toughest years (junior and senior year), I started sharing my whole self with them and expanding my circle of connections with people who liked reading as much as I did. That was liberating. By the end of senior year, I found myself in touch with more people who were into my stuff. Those who didn't see eye to eye with me and my interests had two options: either accept me or leave me. And to my great surprise, most of them accepted me and even became more appreciative of my presence.

Even if you're a big nerd and into fashion and media studies, you need a break from reading and dealing with texts, lines, and scribbling on notebooks. So, music, movies, and TV shows come into the game and show off their greatest benefits. Learning English with music, especially rap, was such a natural thing for me to do. Transitioning from movies and TV shows was also a favorable switch and addition in my learning journey. Not only I was able to enhance my creative writing skills, with a myriad of storylines and narratives that would come off both my brain and the screen, but I was also capable to get the gist, the context, and some real-life experience from the characters. I learned how romantic words would sound if they were ever said to me, how to battle against the bad if I had some superpowers, and how to fantasize about driving a car in a race in the midst of an adventure.

Granted, those were not realistic scenarios, but I could learn a lot from them. I was still the girl who would wake up in the morning and find herself on a college campus with other thousands of students just like her. However, they made me dream while learning, with sounds, colors, and words. This shows the incredible potential of TV shows and movies. If you want to invest in your creativity, I'd highly suggest watching movies and TV shows, in addition to listening to music and reading books. If you think about it, how many times does a conversation start with a quote or a movie reference? How many times did you have to break the ice and make a connection with someone through a movie genre that you shared with the person in front of you? And lastly, how many times have cinematographic productions saved you from boredom?

Like all languages in the world, modern English is the reflection of its speakers. The teaching mechanisms and the assimilation of English will always be influenced by politics and the customs of the people who speak it.

For those living in the Western world, technology comes in handy and can be a great tool to stay focused on our work and connected to each other. Nevertheless, many people in the food or artistic industries are finding themselves in an unexpected struggle, where their income is more unstable than ever, and future plans are in the air. Members of the fashion industry are developing and working on new resources to keep generating products and relevant content that will be pertinent and useful to its consumers.

Yes, we're living in a pandemic. The Western world is having a wake-up call and is reacting to this natural way of things. This situation looks a lot like a Black Mirror episode, or if you're old school I might say Twilight Zone. Well, speaking of cinematography, here are some shows and movies with which you can entertain yourself during this quarantine. You can also learn new topics, cultures, and lifestyles.

All of these are Netflix shows. Some of them can be found only on Netflix US, but that might change in the future.

I want to share with you guys some of the movies and TV shows that have pushed me into the world of fashion journalism. Now that the pandemic has affected us, both financially and psychologically, we must adapt to a new form of normality. Things that we used to see and do won't be part of our daily routine anymore. Comebacks will appear from time to time, but adaptation and flexibility to new platforms, realities, and lifestyles will impact us on a great level.

Some of these shows are expected from me, given my semi-romantic, feminine spirit, but others wouldn't have necessarily a direct link to either fashion or journalism. I solely admire them for their writing.

GOSSIP GIRL

Oh well, this is my piece of cake! An exquisite show if I may tell. Gossip Girl narrates the stories of a bunch of rich kids—Serena, Blair, Nate, Chuck, and Dan—living in New York City. There are a million reasons why I love this show and consider it my favorite. The protagonists in Gossip Girl have nothing to do with the background I grew up with. Location-wise, the series is mostly based in the Upper East Side, with some episodes set in Brooklyn, The Hamptons, Paris, and Los Angeles. I watched this show twice. The first round I watched it all in Italian, followed by a second round in English with subtitles. Gossip Girl was my first TV series to follow with passion and attention. I became attached to it because all the drama and the plot twists were set in one of my favorite cities around the world. If you love fashion, this show is for you. Or at least, you should know about it and probably watch at least one episode.

The show is targeted mostly toward a feminine audience because romance and friendships are the principal dynamics recurrent between the main protagonists. Watching Gossip Girl is like watching the Golden Age of Hollywood and romantic comedies from the mid-2000s.

It's been a long time since I've watched this series, but I clearly remember the most exciting and remarkable anecdotes. Gossip Girl has been part of my adolescence, and it will always save a sweet spot in my heart.

The only thing I wish the writers could have done is to put some melanin on these characters, emphasize the diverse universe that New York is full of. Considering the time in which it was written and the part of society they represent—rich young white kids—I could understand those artistic choices. But it's okay. I know that one day someone will write a melanin-ated version and will give the proper credit to all colors, shapes, and sizes that a cosmopolitan city like the Big Apple represents. That someone will probably be me.

SEX AND THE CITY

Carrie, Miranda, Samantha, and Charlotte are four women in the Big Apple living between a cocktail and a party while juggling and loving men from different backgrounds. Sex is the main ingredient, the key to finding the ultimate romantic relationship.

I started this show during quarantine, when my school closed, and I was still on campus. Just like Gossip Girl, I thought that this would be a very feminine show, full of clichés and drama, which I wanted to avoid. I wanted something fresh and funny, but I was also intrigued. I took the leap and scratched the itch I've always had regarding this show.

When it first aired on the Italian screens, I wasn't allowed to watch it at home. I remember one time my dad giving me a frown when the ads of this show would come on during the commercials. I understand him now, but back then I didn't understand why he was reacting like that. Besides, I wasn't very much into the show because my focus was mostly on That's So Raven and Hannah Montana. So, I let it slide. When I was in middle school and then in high school, more girls knew about this show, but it still wasn't one of my priorities. At thirteen years old, I was still very much into High School Musical. At eighteen, I was hooked into Audrey Hepburn's and Marylin Monroe's cinematography.

Summer 2015 and my last year of high school was a turning point for me. I gave my first kiss on the lips, tried to smoke a cigarette—which I hated and regretted—had my very first sip of absinthe at a bar with my friends, actively and repeatedly listened to rap, and started watching Gossip Girl. Gossip Girl was basically my refuge. Since everyone I knew was aware of my passion for Gossip Girl, they suggested that I watch Sex and the City. "You will love it, it is so you," some of them would say. I honestly never thought that a bunch of white ladies from the Upper East Side would look like me, especially rich women having romance and sex with bold and energetic men. Fast forward to 2019, whenever I would meet Alyssa in her apartment in Queens, we would sometimes talk about boys and our thoughts would spin around and come to different conclusions. Sometimes she would mention the character of Carrie, given our shared passion for writing and reading, along with Miranda and Charlotte. In the same period, I would see a lot of posts and pictures about it on my social media timelines. Still, I wasn't fully interested in getting into the series. However, quarantine kicked in, and here I am in front of HBO wanting to give a chance to the adventures of the four young women looking for the ultimate perfect romantic relationship. I must say that this show has sparked an interest in me. I can see why so many people would see me as Carrie, Charlotte, or Miranda (she is actually my least favorite among all of them), and some of them even as Samantha (my favorite character among all of them).

Despite being a limited production in terms of diversity and queer representation, the structure and the dynamics that are analyzed and explored throughout the episodes engage with an appropriate tone and style typical of a society that is fading more and more. Sex and the City is the testimony of an old class, made of old money, in a city like New York, always changing and in search of novelty. In a world like today, Carrie, Samantha, Charlotte, and Miranda would still exist in their Upper East (if not Upper West) Side apartments, but some of their conversations, their costumes, and communication patterns would drastically change. Watching Sex and the City during this quarantine was not at all a waste of time, but an actual revaluation of what the narratives are around fashion and the media. Those clichés were already on the verge of a drastic change, and now with what COVID-19 pushed, those clichés are historical evidence of an era that we were so used to being in. Now it's time to change. Sex and the City is history. Watching it is like being in an entertainment history class.

THE DEVIL WEARS PRADA
A cult movie, and if you haven't watched this production, what are you waiting for? The Devil Wears Prada is the story about a young woman, Andrea, who by chance enters the fashion industry as an administrative assistant for Miranda

Priestly, a famous fashion editor. This was one of the first movies I watched when I was in my early teens. I remember watching it with my parents, and then alone because it was one of those movies with which I would learn English with the help of subtitles.

This movie, like Sex and the City, Gossip Girl, and other similar productions, glorifies the Manhattan socialites and fashionable characters, who move from place to place but end up professing an incredible love for the city of New York. Have you noticed how the cliché of New York and Paris often surface in these kinds of productions? The parallelism between chaos and pleasure, hardship and love are always constants. I foresee a change in the industry, where they will start considering other places to narrate stories about love—not only romantic love, but also platonic, familiar, and so much more. These movies are models, but I definitely consider them outdated. Who's next?

GROWN-ISH

My heart has been fully invested in Grown-ish since its very first season. Grown-ish is the spinoff series of Kenya Barris' Black-ish. Even though a lot of people have commented on this show by pointing out how unrealistic the scenarios and the relationships in this show are, Grown-ish elevated American romantic comedies on another level, where diversity and representation is appreciated and showcased. The protagonist of this show is Zoey, played by Yara Shahidi. Yara is such a delicate and talented actress, whose humanitarian work and social activism is always on point. I appreciate her sense of fashion and her work in both the fashion and cinema industry.

THE OFFICE AND PARKS AND RECREATION

The Office and Parks and Recreation are solid shows to watch and enjoy. The downside of both relies on how much humor you can get. They also require an excellent understanding of the English language. My slang and phrasal verbs knowledge grew exponentially with these shows. They represent how corporate America works, and how American culture is integrated in everyday life, through an acute humor and sparkling comedic notes.

During my time at Hofstra my English got better and better mostly because of the TV shows and the movies that I would watch between one class and another. If you ask anyone who studied at Hofstra with me, they will tell you many things about me depending on what their relationship is with me, but one thing they will tell you for sure is that I loathed the student center and the cafeteria. These places were always filled with people, and even though I seem like such an extroverted person now, at the very start of my college career I was low-key shy. I wouldn't even use the word "shy." Let's say "modest." I never wanted to draw attention to myself or talk to a lot of people, and sometimes my anxiety would naturally come up, and I would end up losing my appetite. In Italy, I wasn't used to have a multitude of people in just one place during my lunch time. For me, those moments were private, where I would consume my meal with an intimate group of people or simply just alone. Most of my dearest friends didn't have the same schedule as I had either, so we would eat together later in the day. The only time I loved meeting people was at dinner. I liked going out to the cafeteria at the end of the day or even chilling at the student center at late hours. I was also very skeptical around the boys who would approach me in these places. For a long time, I had an inferiority complex, and I wasn't comfortable meeting new people in public places. I would always worry if other people would talk about me chatting with a specific boy, if some sorority girl wanted to start some beef with me, if some people would become envious of me just because I was talking to someone popular. I laugh and smile at the thought of these worries I had in my freshman and sophomore years. I kept not liking the student center for other reasons, but once I realized that being in college is like being on the same sinking boat, I couldn't care less what people think about me. Period.

The shows that would make my day every single day during lunch time were The Office and Parks and Recreation. At the beginning, I wasn't convinced at all that I would like them, especially The Office. The Office narrates the daily routine of the team at a paper company called Dunder Mifflin. The series is set in Scranton, Pennsylvania. Once I grasped the humor of Michael Scott, Jim, Pam, and the others, there was no way back. I became addicted to The Office! After some time, I started watching Parks and Recreation, another gem from Greg Daniels and Michael Schur. If you want to laugh and relax, these are great shows.

NEXT IN FASHION

Well, it's not like Project Runway, but the concept is more or less similar. Hosted by Alexa Chung and Tan France, in this contest show you can learn about fashion, its vocabulary, and the methods and the techniques involved in the industry.

MINIMALISM: A DOCUMENTARY ABOUT THE IMPORTANT THINGS

Almost every person we know aims to purchase and possess items that can help them make their image better, more glamorous, or even more appealing. Objects, clothes, and even books are present in our homes, but do we ever think about how useful they are? Could we live an existence with the bare minimum? Would it be satisfying? Here's a documentary that can help you figure out your answers. As a creative, think: do I need to obtain all these possessions to succeed in life? Is my art or my purpose fulfilled once I own these things?

BOJACK HORSEMAN

Without spoiling anything, BoJack's story is both a remarkable and lame one. He is a typical Hollywood self-centered actor, full of privileges and connections, who encounters challenging and dangerous situations all the time, without realizing right away the best ways to get out of his position. However, he's not a basic character and his actions might find justification in his early childhood. His parents were not the best role models for a son to follow. Young BoJack's innocence brought him far away from that first toxic environment, taking him to the mecca of the arts, Los Angeles. What makes BoJack special is his ability to meet amazing friends and get himself into weird situations. At the end of the show there are some details that I think should've been cleared up better. As a fan of the show I thought that leaving to the viewer's imagination what BoJack's daughter might have thought of him, Todd's life with his girlfriend, and just a sneak peek of Mr. Peanutbutter's life after splitting up with Pickles would've been a cooler move from the writers. On the other hand, Diane's side was elaborated enough to give an idea and finally she deserved the happy ending she needed to have.

BoJack's future seems unsure. His pessimism brought him to many rock bottoms, but his faith in his friends leveled up his quality of life. We can say that at the end of this season he finally realized that it's been quite a journey, but it's time to go on. The best conclusion was defined by Princess Carolyne and Judah, her husband. Yes, I'm sorry, I'll say it: workaholic, caring, lovable, spinster, heartbroken Princess Carolyn marries a man who loves her for who she is and what she does! I loved to see it.

I learned many things from this show. To an extent I laughed at the movie industry in LA, which of course is a big part of the show itself. What struck me in this show were the subtle punchlines that BoJack and other characters, like Diane and Princess Carolyn, would say to each other, especially while arguing or discussing heavy topics. I appreciated the social activism portrayed in many episodes, specifically the issues related to sexism, feminism, and gender equality in the workplace. The mere fact that the universe of BoJack is made of both humans and animals reminded me that the real world is full of diverse people, so our natures differ a lot from each other. The addition of the animals highlights the idea of diversity, in my opinion. I think that it was a nice touch.

Okay then. BoJack Horseman will probably stop to get in trouble now. At least he didn't disappear . . . or die . . . or . . .

You should watch this series. You can learn about yourself while laughing and smiling a lot if you like dark humor, of course. And if you like messy, complicated stories with a touch of liquor, drama, and smoke, watch BoJack Horseman.

INSECURE

I've caught up with HBO's series Insecure, by Issa Rae. I must admit that my friends were right in telling me to get on it because Issa's adventures are pretty much the kind of material I can get along with.

Insecure is the story of an African American millennial named Issa who lives in Los Angeles, where she has a solid group of friends and a job in community service, which she would be able to enjoy more if the environments she comes across would be filled with more empathetic and understanding people. Issa is a vulnerable but resilient woman, who wants to be loved passionately and respectfully. The show now has four seasons, with a fifth one on its way. Usually the episodes last thirty minutes, produced by a team mostly made up of African Americans and Brown professional creatives. I appreciate the diversity and the intersectionality of the topics discussed in this show.

In Insecure, Issa's best friend is Molly, a successful lawyer in the Los Angeles scene. Molly differs from Issa in temperament and lifestyle. Molly is money-oriented and a workaholic, whereas Issa likes taking her time to figure out what she likes or and doesn't like. Molly is in search of the perfect love and uses her dating life as an escape to not solve her inner issues. Issa enjoys her dating life, but she frequently gets into complicated situations due to her insecurities and weaknesses.

Even though their differences are outstanding, Molly and Issa are chosen sisters who complement each other. However, when life gets in the way and pushes new trajectories, the two women face reality.

In the series, Issa and Molly are in their late twenties and early thirties. They have already been through their post graduate years, full of novelty in adulthood and fresh habits to start from scratch. Issa and Molly are grown women who, under bigger circumstances they couldn't control, face their own differences and wonder if it's worth it to keep such friendship.

Despite the age difference, I have lived, and I am currently living this situation with a few friends from college. Now that we have all graduated, are we going to stay in touch? Was college just a bump, or are we going to keep our connection even during young adulthood? While I was watching the last two episodes of Insecure, I saw in Molly's and Issa's relationship a reflection of some of my dearest college friendships. We have touched the final destination, and now we'll either keep in touch or just let our existences vanish from each other, no matter how harsh it sounds.

During college I haven't had many radical changes of personality, but my style and lifestyle have changed exponentially. These changes were mostly responses to what I was living during that period or to the people I was around. After four years, I can say that I've experienced a vast spectrum of styles and tastes, which expanded my preferences a great deal. I had to say "no" many times to keep firm the best and most vital parts of my lifestyle, as well as to add richer and fuller human connections in my existence. Many friends had to come and go. Did it hurt? Yes. Was it worth it? Most of the time, yes.

Insecure shows that part of the City of Angels that is often underrated in movies or TV shows. Unfortunately, out of the many places she mentions in the show, I only know the most famous ones. My first trip to Los Angeles was a good one, but it was just a tasteful introduction to the most glamorous and golden city on the West Coast. I'm sure that next time will be different. Issa's directions and production do a good job in depicting such a complex city like Los Angeles.

What is incredible about Issa is her ability to turn her initial web-series project, Awkward Black Girl, into a nationally broadcast TV show. I admire her for that. Her hard work has paid off immensely. She is nothing but an inspiration, especially in the Black community. She was one of the first Black creatives I've come across on my own, outside the college walls, during freshman year.

The reality depicted in Insecure's dynamics between Issa and Molly is significant and speaks volumes, especially about young women. Our behaviors can be so engulfed in matters that hurt us, but we don't realize the consequences until we face them once and for all. When we're given an ultimatum in a friendship everything can change, either for the best or for the worst. In the end, you'll still always have yourself, but if you happen to break that meaningful bond, what happens next? Will your choices save or destroy you?

If you stay true to yourself and are comfortable within your own peace, everything will work in your favor. But once disrespect and lack of communication creeps in, it's time to move on and accept what a certain friendship has been throughout the years. It served a purpose, it was cyclic, and it has come to its end.

I can't wait to see what happens next on Insecure. Meanwhile, I can't wait to see what will happen to my next platonic relationships. I'll see which ones will be worth keeping and which ones are destined to fade away.

CHAPTER 7

THE BEATS

Dear readers,

Amid all the recent unexpected and shaking events in 2020, I have taken time to reevaluate the lessons learned during these last four years. Phases in life come and go and have their own waves of frequencies. Some periods are tough, others are sweeter, and so on. Despite the great number of shifts that a person might experience, the constant element that keeps growing is self-love, as long as someone gives it a shot. For me self-love is still a journey. I concluded that self-love will always be my first and foremost trip to embark on, no matter when or where I'll be in life. I have to work on and let go of so many things, but without a doubt I can affirm now that my passions come from a place of curiosity, love, and empathy. For some reason, especially during those times when I felt the loneliest and most misunderstood, I would find total solace in music.

See, here's the thing: I don't like wasting time. If there's something that gets on my nerves the most, it's being bored while doing nothing. Many of my friends in college would get bored so easily, and I would lose my temper or simply get annoyed by the lack of enthusiasm they were showing. With time and patience, I got better at managing my company, skimming through the right people to hang out with, and the ones to care the most about. Music and fashion became my personal spaces on campus because they were engaging and welcoming with their visuals and sounds.

As a communications major, my classes, homework, and extracurricular activities were focused solely on words. I attended journalism courses, literature classes, writing workshops, and creative writing laboratories. To unplug my brain and rest my eyes, I needed to rely on other kinds of media. I was tired of reading or sitting in front of a computer after my classes. I wanted to listen rather than read, or if I had enough strength in my eyes, scroll on my Instagram to watch a fashion show or look at a soothing aesthetic page. In this way, I thought, I would relax, but not lose any time at all. Productivity is key to success.

Along with my interest in music, I would discover new songs and artists every week for almost two years. Rap, trap, soca, and reggae made me think about my repressed childhood moments, the part of my life that for a long time had been closed and clogged with other genres and streams of media. I listened to a lot of classical music during my teens, and for four years those tunes were put aside. I wanted to prioritize what I had missed during my teens and get on the same level as my American peers. In fact, just before moving to the U.S., I had written my first motto. It was my first Instagram biography: "I'm more of a Gershwin fan, but Macklemore once said: 'The quickest way to happiness?

Learning to be selfless.'"[22] With these words I wanted to launch a very specific message, which was: "I might listen to jazz or older genres, but there's a great message and importance in other genres too. I'm open to embrace new experiences, sounds, and views."

At first, particularly during freshman year, all I wanted to do was to learn about names like Chance the Rapper, Jhené Aiko, Wale, or Kehlani, simply because I didn't want to attend a party or be part of a conversation and zone out when they would ask me my opinion on "Chance's new album," "Jhené's last single," or "Kehlani's fresh collaboration."

It all started from a place of curiosity. I had no intention of becoming fully invested and in admiration of the new artists and music I was coming across. I just wanted to expand my horizons and appreciate new sounds. I had to listen again to the sounds that I had listened to back home with my mom and my family in Brazil, sounds that got lost while I was in Italy. The exposure to music, except for classical, rock, pop, or jazz, was limited among my friends in Florence. At home I only had my mom to exchange musical tastes and engage conversations around music with. Listening to various music genres was difficult with my dad. He would stick to only his favorite genres and not dig into others.

My parents are a bit old school when it comes to music, even my mom who's more flexible in giving an ear for new sounds. My dad listens to rock and doesn't know anything about rap; my mom listens to bossa nova and doesn't like

---

22   Macklemore ft. Ed Sheeran, "Growing Up (Sloane's song)."

Brazilian funk. However, that didn't stop me from going out and discovering new, modern, fresh sounds, especially with my peers. Still, my friends only knew Italian music and some rap, and for some reason, I wasn't hooked to those artists at first because I had no context or space to explore this type of music and complement them with other sounds of preference: jazz, classical, and samba songs. Fast forward four years, I finally found the right environments in which I could listen to, appreciate, and learn from these genres, even among other Italians and Brazilians. Now I finally found a place in my head and spirit where I can blend all these beats.

Once I dove into popular culture through my writing and civic engagement studies, it was inevitable to incorporate the fashion world and study, analyze, and learn everything on the designs, the stylists, and the myriad of styles that America has within its territories. Music and fashion became intertwined and the inner child in me, that little person who would always sing and dance in front of either the TV or my parents' mirror, started wondering about writing music videos, directing photoshoots, and combining visuals, sounds, and words in one place. My old hyperactivity was translated into a new form of mental energy. It was inescapable to not be inspired by music and ultimately combine all the sounds I knew in my homework, writing, and life.

Music and fashion were the protagonists of my leisure time; things that I could learn from and relax with simultaneously. For someone who doesn't like to sit around and do nothing and always wants to learn, this is a great way to balance your life. Despite my hunger for knowledge—and unfortunately sometimes perfectionism—I bumped my head many times.

I keep learning that doing nothing is actually good from time to time. I'm getting better at not having panic attacks or anxious moments whenever things slow down. I am just enjoying myself, taking two bites more of a scrumptious cupcake, closing my eyes and listening to the wind, or just looking up at the sky. I found out that I actually learn a lot from these dull moments too.

In four years, my ears have listened to an amplified music catalog. I caught new melodies, amazing lyrics, and enchanting productions in many languages and from different cultures. I always have a hard time when I'm asked what my favorite song is or who my favorite artist is because I have so many talented people on my mind. Usually, I tend to give more space to female voices rather than male ones, but there's a very small difference between the two genders. I switch from pop to jazz, or from rap to classical pretty fast because my mind is a stream of consciousness. However, whenever my body needs its relaxation, I make sure to play the right music to set a mood. On the other hand, without hesitation I blast my sounds with active and bumping beats when my body demands the energy that it requires.

My journey in discovering fashion and journalism has encountered several beats, which have inspired, soothed, and calmed me during the most beautiful and painful times. These songs made me laugh, fall in love, dance, dream, and cry, and restored my spirit. I would like to share with you some of the songs that have accompanied me on this journey. The beats, lyrics, and productions (music videos included) say a lot about me. They say what kind of millennial I am, how I am entering adulthood with a hint of joy and bittersweetness, but with mostly joy and gratitude for all the feelings I've been able to experience and live through. Let the beats roll!

1. LCD Soundsystem–New York, I Love You but You're Bringing Me Down
2. Outkast–Prototype
3. Lauryn Hill–Doo Wop (That Thing)
4. Marvin Gaye ft. Tammi Terrell–Ain't No Mountain High Enough
5. Corinne Bailey Rae–Put Your Records On
6. Mutya Buena–Real Girl
7. Leon Bridges–Lisa Sawyer
8. Tyler, The Creator–See You Again
9. Juice WRLD–Lucid Dreams
10. Mac Miller ft. Ariana Grande–My Favorite Part
11. Saweetie–ICY GIRL
12. Kash Doll–Doin Too Much
13. Frankie Valli–Can't Take My Eyes Off You
14. Big Sean–One Man Can Change the World
15. Danileigh–Easy
16. Rosalia ft. Ozuna–Yo X Ti, Tu X Por Mi
17. J. Balvin and Bad Bunny–QUE PRETENDES
18. Bad Bunny–Solo de Mi
19. oui - Jeremih
20. David Bowie–Modern Love
21. The Jackson 5–Who's Lovin' You
22. Rocco Hunt–Tutto resta
23. Cardi B–Please Me
24. Jack Harlow–What's Poppin
25. Mustard–Ballin'
26. Roddy Rich–High Fashion

27. Noname–Diddy Bop
28. Noname–Shadow Man
29. Pixote–Nem de Graça
30. Snoop Dogg ft. Pharrell Williams–Beautiful
31. Dave–Location
32. Burna Boy–Gum Body
33. Kiana Lede'–Wicked Games
34. Sade–Your Love Is King
35. Paul Anka–Put Your Head on My Shoulder
36. The Ronettes–Be My Baby
37. Wale–Lotus Flower Bomb
38. Nelly ft. Kelly Rowland–Dilemma
39. Logic–1-800-273-8255
40. Mary J. Blige–Be Without You
41. Destiny's Child–Girl
42. Nivea–Laundromat
43. Elton John and Kiki Dee–Don't Go Breaking My Heart
44. Noemi–Sono solo parole
45. Elisa–Eppure sentire (un senso di te)
46. Coez–E' sempre bello
47. Stromae–Formidable
48. Bow Wow ft. Ciara–Like You
49. Norah Jones–Don't Know Why
50. Dreamville–Under The Sun
51. Michael Bublé–It's a Beautiful Day
52. Michael Jackson–PYT
53. John Legend–PDA
54. PARTYNEXTDOOR (with Drake and Bad Bunny)–LOYAL
55. Stormzy ft. Lily Allen and Kehlani–Cigarettes and Cush
56. Drake–Signs
57. Drake–Controlla
58. Drake ft Jhene Aiko–From Time

59. Drake–Chicago Freestyle
60. Drake–Best I Ever Had
61. Cesare Cremonini–La Nuova Stella di Broadway
62. Cesare Cremonini–Poetica
63. Jorja Smith–Lost & Found
64. Jorja Smith–Where Did I Go?
65. Annalisa–Questo bellissimo gioco
66. Annalisa–Una finestra tra le stelle
67. Chance the Rapper–Same Drugs
68. Chance the Rapper ft. Noname–Israel
69. Chance the Rapper–Cocoa Butter Kisses
70. Carl Brave x Franco 126–Sempre In Due
71. Carl Brave x Franco 126–Argentario
72. Carl Brave–Fotografia
73. Olly Murs–Dance With Me Tonight
74. Vinicius De Morais–Samba da benção
75. Gilberto Gil–Aos Pes da Santa Cruz
76. Antonio Carlos Jobim and Elis Regina–Triste
77. Antonio Carlos Jobim–Corcovado
78. Antonio Carlos Jobim and Elis Regina–Aguas De Marco
79. Rihanna–Work
80. Rihanna–Love On The Brain
81. Rihanna–Higher
82. Tiziano Ferro–Eri Come L'oro Ora Sei Come Loro
83. Tiziano Ferro–Hai delle isole negli occhi
84. Tiziano Ferro–Ti scattero' una foto
85. Tiziano Ferro–Ed ero contentissimo
86. Tiziano Ferro–Accetto Miracoli
87. Kanye West–Heartless
88. Kanye West–Lamborghini Mercy
89. Kanye West–Touch The Sky
90. Jay-Z, Chrisette Michele – Lost One

91. Jay Z–Excuse Me Miss
92. Jay Z–The Story of O.J.
93. Jhene Aiko–None Of Your Concerns
94. Jhene Aiko–July
95. Jhene Aiko–Spotless Mind
96. Jhene Aiko–B.S.
97. Jhene Aiko–10K Hours
98. Megan Thee Stallion–Cash Shit
99. Megan Thee Stallion–Captain Hook
100. Megan Thee Stallion–Savage
101. Mariah Carey–We Belong Together
102. Mariah Carey–It's Like That
103. Black Eyed Peas–Don't Lie
104. Da Baby–BOP
105. Da Baby–VIBEZ
106. Ghali–Cara Italia
107. Ghali–Happy Days
108. Solange–Don't Touch My Hair
109. Solange–Almeda
110. Chloe X Halle (ft. Joey Badass)–Happy Without Me
111. Janelle Monae–Make Me Feel
112. Lady Gaga–Paparazzi
113. Beyonce'–Me, Myself, and I
114. Beyonce'–Hold Up
115. Beyonce'–XO
116. Taylor Swift–New Romantics
117. Taylor Swift–Style
118. Taylor Swift–Starlight
119. Jovanotti–Le Tasche Piene Di Sassi
120. Jovanotti–Punto
121. Jovanotti–Serenata rap

122. Anika Noni Rose–Almost There
 (from The Princess and the Frog)
123. Kendrick Lamar–Bitch, Don't Kill My Vibe
124. Ariana Grande–My Everything
125. Ariana Grande–Dangerous Woman
126. Ariana Grande–Let Me Love You
127. Ariana Grande–imagine
128. Ariana Grande–successful
129. Ilene Woods and Mike Douglas (from Cinderella)
 –So This Is Love
130. Pink Floyd–Wish You Were Here
131. Rick Ross ft. Drake–Gold Roses
132. Stockard Channing–There Are Worse Things
 I Could Do (from Grease)
133. Justin Timberlake–Mirrors
134. Summer Walker (ft. Jhene Aiko)–I'll Kill You
135. Summer Walker - Body
136. Emma Watson (from Beauty and the Beast)–Belle
137. Alicia Keys–You Don't Know My Name
138. Alicia Keys–Jane Doe
139. Alicia Keys–Girlfriend
140. Alicia Keys–If I Ain't Got You
141. Alicia Keys–Unbreakable
142. Kali Uchis–Loner
143. Kali Uchis–honey baby (SPOILED!)
144. Kali Uchis ft. Tyler The Creator–After The Storm
145. Kali Uchis ft. Jorja Smith–Tyrant
146. Kali Uchis–Flight 22
147. Childish Gambino–3005
148. Childish Gambino–Baby Boy
149. Childish Gambino–Redbone
150. Childish Gambino–Sober

151. Childish Gambino–Summertime Magic
152. Macklemore ft. Ed Sheeran–Growing Up
    (Sloan's song)
153. Macklemore & Ryan Lewis–Kevin
154. Bruno Mars–Locked out of Heaven
155. Bruno Mars ft. Cardi B–Finesse
156. Bruno Mars–Straight up & Down
157. The Beatles–I Want To Hold Your Hand
158. The Beatles–Day Tripper
159. The Beatles–In My Life
160. The Beatles–Hey Jude
161. Bas, J. Cole - Tribe
162. Ciara–Body Party
163. Elijah Kelley–Run And Tell That
164. Zac Efron, Elijah Kelley, Nikki Blonsky, Amanda
    Bynes from Hairspray–Without Love
165. Lana Del Rey–Video Games
166. Lana Del Rey–Brooklyn Baby
167. Lana Del Rey–Bel Air
168. Lana Del Rey–Black Beauty
169. Lana Del Rey–Once Upon a Dream from Maleficent
170. Lana Del Rey–Young and Beautiful from The Great Gatsby
171. Khalid–Talk
172. Lukas Graham–Funeral
173. Lukas Graham–Strip No More
174. Lizzo–Good As Hell
175. Lizzo–Coconut Oil
176. Amy Winehouse–Like Smoke
177. Amy Winehouse–Tears Dry On Their Own
178. Amy Winehouse–Rehab
179. Amy Winehouse–Me & Mr. Jones
180. Amy Winehouse–Take The Box

181. Amy Winehouse–I Heard Love Is Blind
182. H.E.R.- Best Part
183. H.E.R.–Focus
184. Ella Mai–Gut Feeling
185. Ella Mai–Boo'd Up
186. Kehlani–Piece of Mind
187. Kehlani–Love Language
188. Kehlani–Can I
189. Lil Wayne - How To Love
190. Tyler, The Creator – FUCKING YOUNG/PERFECT
191. Roy Ayers Ubiquity–Everybody Loves the sunshine
192. Nicki Minaj–Pills 'n Potions
193. Nicki Minaj–Barbie Dreams
194. Nicki Minaj–Super Bass
195. Melanie Martinez–Alphabet Boy
196. Melanie Martinez–High School Sweethearts
197. A$AP Rocky - Fashion Killa
198. Frank Ocean–Thinkin Bout You
199. Frank Ocean–Moon River
200. Frank Ocean–Pink + White

CONCLUSION
- AN OPEN LETTER TO
FRESH BEGINNINGS

———

Dear readers,

I still remember the day when Trump was nominated President of the United States in November 2016. By the following month I had seen many tears being shed down my peers' faces. I didn't understand why crying was an innate response to politics. How bad could this guy could be? I thought. He doesn't look good, but he can't be that bad. His behavior must be just an exaggeration. I was thinking this because I had never questioned the American Dream, the lifestyle that everyone from all over the world aspires to. How could the president of the country of the ultimate dream crush this iconic pillar and landmark, something that every immigrant longs for? And here I am, almost four years later living my dream: a dream in a dreadful nightmare.

Besides my personal life, which was going to be chaotic anyways during these times, the world is the protagonist of an unexpected simulation, a dystopian Black Mirror episode. If you're a young Brown woman in media who just graduated from college, an Italian-Brazilian living in the U.S., under a pandemic and a series of racist events, there's only one single thing you can think of and agree on: what a time to be alive.

Numerology and cataclysms were the most popular features of 2020. It was in fact a leap year with remarkable people passing away from January until May under a pandemic and with outbursts of several civil rights movements, especially Black Lives Matter.

The death of George Floyd didn't surprise me. Police brutality has been a reality that I had to accept and digest, in addition to questioning it and learning about it. When I first arrived at Hofstra, I had a different idea of what racism was like in the U.S. I thought that everything was solved after Martin Luther King's activism, Rosa Parks' actions, Angela Davis' efforts, and Malcom X's responses. No more racism, at least the history books said so. I had done my homework.

In Italy we're not taught how the States are in contemporary times. We're just starting right now to have more transparent conversations, where non-white Italians are taking more space on media, as well as the queer and plus-size communities. We grasp information from movies, TV shows, songs, toys, media, and magazines. What's glorified in the U.S. is glorified elsewhere. With the advent of social media, journalists, writers, and celebrities write about what's happening in the U.S. and use their words to report the facts. See

Francesco Costa with his podcast and newsletter Da Costa a Costa, Federico Rampini from La Repubblica, Afroitalian Souls and its founders, and the digital collective Kube, led by Ludovica Narciso.

Even if I'd had a father who was always reading The New Yorker and having discussions with me about American politics, I couldn't fully understand and see the issues that the modern USA has been facing, especially if we're talking about minorities. Coming from a predominantly white country, it is not surprising to receive partial news, media, movies, and so on. However, it didn't take me a lot of time to comprehend the real picture and the ugly scenarios that non-white people live with in this country.

I had entered this country with an Italian, white mind even though I am Brown. It wasn't a matter of hate or standing against an idea. I was simply misinformed, naive, and confined in a bubble. I didn't grow up with many Black Italians. My mom never had race conversations with me at home in Italy, even though I was exposed to those types of arguments anytime I would be in Brazil, with my relatives who are educators and social activists. Despite these episodes, my Black mom shared only her own experience with me, but it clearly wasn't like the ones that an African American woman lives. Naturally, it is different although being Black is a universal experience per se. However, at home, in my town, or in any other part of the nation, I was never perceived as a threat. In Italy, we don't have the n-word with the same weight and connotations, and we never had a history of slavery like the U.S. or other European colonies. But it's just incredible that I was able to find this cultural and ethnical equilibrium in myself in a country that was neither Brazil nor Italy. A country that I oddly call "home," maybe because "home" is a state of mind.

I thought that my skin color was an ugly feature only when it came to boys, to whom I was never a good-looking choice. At the end of the day, I believed that I was just like my Black and Brown peers in America. I would watch them in movies and music videos: shiny, glamorous, with the latest hairstyle, with a boyfriend or girlfriend. Everything that I couldn't see myself having or experiencing in Italy was in America. My American Dream was to be in a country where people who look like me can be appreciated and loved for what they do and believe. Once I landed here, I came to understand more and more those sporadic conversations my mom and her family had shared with me in Brazil, in the hood. Even my father's words started making more sense. But until then, nobody had instructed me that my skin color could put me in absurd danger, from going to jail to being shot on a sidewalk by a police officer. I had to learn this by myself, both through an academic context and unforgettable friendships.

The death of George Floyd is a murder. It shocked me because for the very first time I thought, "That could've been my friend." A man who had minor penalties but served a deadly sentence. That could have been my homie. What disgusts me is not only the inhumanity that public authorities and narrow-minded white people display, but also the systematic racism that this country still perpetuates, no matter how often and constantly its people keep fighting to abolish these atrocities. I just go by logic: how does a country built by immigrants attack similar people? At the end of the day, what does the color of skin change? What's the deal with someone's skin complexion? I love both my dad and mom, white and Black. My white and non-white friends. And I am not saying we're the same, but that's what I love about the world.

As a biracial person, having experienced Trump's presidency was a roller coaster of emotions, because I simply couldn't understand his motives in conducting such a racist and inaccurate agenda. The more time I spent with my professors, friends, coworkers, and mentors, the deeper my analysis and feelings toward this country grew. In four years, my answers and opinions haven't changed, only empowered and enriched. I still find it absurd that people like Trayvon Martin, Michael Brown, Breonna Taylor, and so many other souls were murdered. Black souls.

As I've wrapped up my college journey, I took time to think about the people I got the chance to meet during these last four years. A great portion, if not most of my American friends are POC, most of them Black. I am so grateful for their friendships because they were all I wanted back home. Girls who could get my hair and share secrets, concerns, and stories, as well as remarkable experiences. Guys that were brothers to me, best friends, and some of them even lovers have changed my life. They showed me the world of rap and the world of fashion (even though I come from one of the most renowned places in fashion). With my best American girlfriends, I have learned to become an independent woman, to embrace my beauty, struggles, failures, and victories. They were like older sisters.

Sometimes I think about my future and the possibility of having a family. My kids will be Black, regardless of who I have kids with. Their mother will need to help them navigate this world and if I happen to stay here in the U.S., then I need to know myself and my position in society. The thought of having kids is still something surreal. I am actually scared of babies, I feel awkward holding them, and sometimes even babysitting them if they're too young. But having conversations with older friends of mine who are starting families, are in committed relationships, or are thinking about adopting a kid make me think about endless futures I could have. Regardless of what I will happen to be in or have in my life, I will always need to embrace my biracial background, my marvelous Brown skin, and my voluptuous 3C hair. Journalist or not, screenwriter or not, creative director or not, model or not, single or not, all of these conversations and news matter to me.

My heart is heavy, because the love I have for me and those dear ones is full and charged. Even though these are hard times, I am glad I still have my own body that stands still and firm. My fingers are ready to type fast and report what is necessary. My eyes scroll from screen to screen, line to line, and absorb all they can. My ears lean to both weak and strong voices, rhythmic verses, and heart-aching melodies. My heart carries a lot of emotions and affections. The only safe place my most sincere feelings can be now is just my heart. A heavy muscle pumping and keeping its lively beats.

Sometimes I think that I'm still not good enough to start a project, a career path, or anything creative. However, I have concluded that this is the time when I can only start doing something. There's nothing else I can finish, since I am growing out from my old experiences, biological phases, and school years. These worries and fears are inevitable because I'm not going to lie: I'm so hungry to write and produce high quality content, to work with amazing people, and live my life at full capacity. I need money, a solid network, and good vibes for that. I need accountability and positivity too! In college I've struggled to keep up with these goals. Now I feel like I'm closer to what I want to get, but there's always the fear that I feel like I'm behind, not good enough, I'll always be a learner and never a master. But the thing is that I've got tons to offer. I've started from scratch, with no help from Mom, Dad, relatives, connections in the field, and not even friends when I first came to the U.S. All I've done has been done by me, period. It's hard, but I hope one day to see the fruits! And with those fruits I'll make a hell of a salad bowl. No pineapples or kiwis though, I'm allergic.

I was scared of the idea of writing this book. When Professor Koester told me about his project with New Degree Press, I felt both honored and anxious. I kept thinking about why I would be the right person to start working on such a project. Why would someone choose me to write a book while in college, in the midst of exams, homework, and still figuring out who I am? Well, this book probably came out at the right time. I can say this only with hindsight. I started thinking about my stories and how much I have always wished to have someone who looked like me, telling these kinds of stories, or at least being able to narrate like an older sister or a mom would, with gentle and straightforward tones. This book signified a spiritual journey for me, one that life forces you to take when facing and exploring your emotions. This is a small book, but it has a big message: the willingness to be present, learn, and love yourself.

Four major events shaped me in the last four years: my first day of college in 2016, my first day of my sophomore year in 2017, one random day in July 2018, and one random day in October 2019. All these dates have a significant importance in my personal life, and they had a huge impact on my personality. They brought me immense joy in the most unexpected ways. They brought me new friends and lovers. They made me discover different versions of myself, fresh pleasures, and new interests in my life. The stories that happened after each of these events have been heartbreaking, incredible, blessed, and constructive. Tears of joy and sadness have flowed from my eyes on so many occasions. However, the young woman I am today is the result of the love developed in herself, whose perception and sensibility has been profoundly sharpened. I always wonder if I ever will have days like these. I used to think about how I'm so lucky to have lived such feelings, and why the best of them had to fade away. Probably the last part is what makes them so special and dear in my heart.

Many would think the opposite, but music was the medium that helped me get back and stick to journalism. There was a time in fact when I wanted to ditch everything and everyone. I didn't feel worthy of any love at all. I felt like a failure in every aspect of my life and my passions weren't sustaining me anymore. The biggest mistake I made in that context was to not give myself enough credit and love for the work I was doing at the time. My thirst to be on point and reach my dreams was so big that I had forgotten to actually enjoy the present moment. I loved passion, but I wasn't getting the point of it. I loved a person, but I wasn't being present in their life. I wanted to be like my friends in the city, but I didn't consider the ones closer to me. That touch of ambition I was adding in my life with the lack of self-love I was carrying around on my shoulders was the cherry on the top of the cake. At some point, all the things I cared about turned toxic. And the only solution I could see for myself was to just escape, disappear, and eventually not live anymore. However, music became the shelter. Audio platforms like podcasts and radio shows made me feel less lonely. Because of the internet and the art of music, I was able to find an old passion of mine, listening to music. I had lost the capacity and the curiosity to tune in with the music I used to listen to.

I started listening to Italian music, from my childhood songs to the newest releases, British music, like The Beatles and Amy Winehouse, and Brazilian music, especially bossa nova. My tastes started to expand more and more, and I ended up with old school rap, like Tupac, Biggie, Eminem, and Latino-pop music, with artists like Bad Bunny and Kali Uchis. Through each song's lyrics I was able to get in sync with my old self, remind my spirit about my origins, and explore different musical genres. Getting interested in music and its production made me want to read about music production, music history, and similar topics. It was a way to escape from fashion and all the other things I was passionate about. Despite my desire to erase my love towards fashion, journalism, and everyone close to me, music pushed me in the opposite direction. The music industry is very much linked to the fashion industry. Many singers and rappers own a style and have a story to tell in their songs, in their beats, and in their melodies. All these elements made me go back to writing and eventually into fashion. Music was the tool that both distracted and instructed me to keep pushing my creativity and end up again with dear loves of mine: fashion journalism, and writing about visuals, art, social justice, and representation in media.

I haven't written this book to prove anything, but to share everything. My intention is to show you how powerful creativity can be within our adversities. Going through personal hard times and events like COVID-19 have shaped me a great deal. I am for sure a new person right now at the moment of writing these words. I feel woke and definitely more energetic and surer of my capabilities. Some may say I'm not innocent or naive or optimistic like I once was. Some might believe my heart is closed, and that I don't trust anyone anymore. Some will probably think that I'm "too much" or "not enough." But my creative persona was able to shut down these thoughts and opinions and push through my purpose. I am ready.

I wanted to share with you a sort of Q&A that I've featured in one of my blog posts, on thecurlyflower.com, for the collective Celeste Journal (@celeste.journal on Instagram).

INTRODUCE YOURSELF

My name is Giulia. I go also by "**the curly flower.**" I'm a journalist, writer, fashion model, and student of life. Yes, I learn both in school and in the streets. That's how life goes, at least the best ones. I practice my job by voicing social matters and writing on fashion. I love my hair and my curls. I sleep with a teddy bear named John. I've had him since I was eight years old. I love drinking tea and eating blueberries. I also love chocolate. Oh my, my addiction to chocolate is bad.

HOW DID YOU FIND YOUR WAY INTO WRITING?
DID YOU ALWAYS WANTED TO BE A WRITER?

My first dream job was to become a ballerina at my prestigious local theatre, and I remember wishing to be the first Brown ballerina to dance on the stage. That dream job didn't realize itself, but the goal is always there: my wish to see someone who looks like me **on stage**, **on screens** and **on books**, in the arts. I found writing through reading because the latter was my natural and most accessible escape I could afford, especially in the summertime. I started writing and thinking about writing as a career when I was twelve years old, when I was given my first personal notebook: a pink glittery one with a big "High School Musical" title written in capital letters – yes, like the **Disney Channel movie**.

WHY DO YOU WRITE? WHO DO YOU WRITE FOR?
DO YOU HAVE A MESSAGE IN YOUR WORK?

I write to express myself, but I like to see myself as a bridge between one ear and another, one eye and another, in whatever community I happen to be surrounded. I write for the general audience because the goal I plan to achieve through my words is to represent the underrepresented.

IS WRITING WHO YOU ARE OR WHAT YOU DO?

Writing is who I am. It happens to be something that I do too. My words and phrases are moved by love, the love to be present and give time to report and craft stories.

INSPIRATION: WHAT INFLUENCES YOUR WORK THE MOST?

Life. Literally anything I come across. Trips inspire me most because those are the times where I'm forced to rely on and feel unapologetically me, with no filters. Being outside of a comfort zone or in a place I don't know pushes me to pay attention to every single detail and to the people I interact with.

WHAT ARE A FEW WRITERS THAT YOU ADMIRE?

I admire writers not only for their work but also for their **personality and transparency**. Coming from a journalism background, I admire more the words and the story itself rather than just one person's writing. However, in classical literature I admire Louisa May Alcott, Jane Austen, Manzoni, Foscolo, and Dante Alighieri. I grew up with these peeps. Old folks, I know. I have read them by taking into consideration their time and place in history, but I've always wondered if their stories could actually have some melanin in them, if they could be narrated differently, with modern and colorful scenarios. They challenged me in making me go forward within the world I used to live in, predominantly white. Their words and my imagination were the perfect combo, but it wasn't enough. I wanted to see more people working like I wanted to work.

Right now, I don't have any favorite writer. There are amazing fashion writers, whose descriptive and invested vocabulary I look up to, like Elizabeth Cline or Elaine Welteroth, but also many other journalists and talented creative writers, like Vinicius Grossos, Lane Moore, Derek Blesberg, Francesco Costa, etc. Their works and reportages are remarkable and have shaped me a lot. However, I consider part of my reading experience listening and reading music artists' lyrics, which most of the time happen to be poets and writers themselves. Jhene Aiko, Lana Del Rey, Tupac, Joao Gilberto are some of the greatest. A dream of mine would be to be a songwriter. Imagine collaborating with either Jhene Aiko or Lana Del Rey and turn one of my poems into a song, with their melodies and vibes: oh, how lit it would be!

YOUR FAVORITE BOOKS? FILM?

I don't have a favorite book because reading is a temporary activity with permanent consequences. If I would read a book two or three times, I would see that work with a different and more mature mindset. That happened with my favorite movie, Breakfast at Tiffany's, which I learned to view the good and the bad that is portrayed in that film. Every time I watch it, I would notice something that I'd both agree and disagree more on. Holly Golightly's character living the life she's living and her reasonings behind it for example: they become clearer and distant, reliable and understandable at the same time.

WHAT IS AN IDEAL PLACE FOR YOU TO EXIST IN?

Anywhere close to the sun. Whether it influences me a lot, I'm not gonna lie. One of my favorite places on Earth is San Juan, in Puerto Rico.

DO YOU HAVE ANY FEMINIST IDEALS YOU WOULD LIKE TO SHARE WITH US?

Rihanna. She really sticks up for what feminism means. I relate and take a lot of my inspiration from the music world because its industry is more fluid in terms of expressions and art creation. There are still many stigmas and misconceptions around it, but it is an astonishing platform from which you can learn. I didn't even think twice while answering this question because for me she embraces femininity in all her shades and shapes. I'm fortunate to live during the same time as she, so that I can see her rising and enjoying her life.

WOULD YOU SAY THAT YOUR WORK IS FEMINIST?

Yes. Or should I say womanist? I'm trying to find the best label that describes my beliefs. I believe in equality, equity, and meritocracy. Is there an adjective for that?

WOULD YOU SAY THAT YOUR WORK IS REPRESENTATIONAL AND IS THAT NECESSARY?

Without doubt. I may sound repetitive in stating my goals, but I put a lot of weight in my words. I try to make them sound **light and easy** to comprehend but always with a **clear and meaningful** message in them. Any work of art made from words, images and forms are necessary or at least valid in their existence.

WHAT IS YOUR RELATIONSHIP TO YOUR BEAUTY? TO YOUR BODY? TO YOUR WOMANHOOD? TO WOMEN?

I wouldn't be honest if I said I've never struggled with my body or the concept of beauty. I've been very much influenced by the trends that the environment I was in had as standards. For example, in Italy I've always longed for thin legs, with less curves in my hip area. In Brazil I would be considered too athletic and "small." When I arrived in the

U.S. I felt more at ease because I could see a mixture of body types. When I entered in the fashion industry, there was a time I thought I was too fat or sometimes too short, but that depended a lot on the kind of groups I was in, especially at the beginning. All these harsh judgements on my body and views that I had were coming from a place of deep insecurity, which I got rid of once I started being focused on my mind rather than my body. The big chop I did was essential to enter this journey of mine, where self-appreciation and health were priorities. I saw an upgrade not only in my mind and physical body, but also in my writing. I'm able to say all of this also because I've decided to be surrounded by women who are my friends. I started valuing spaces where I felt welcomed and loved for who I am, and that was magical. That saved me, tons. I was able to see beautiful things and meet beautiful people through the power of the kindest words: there's what beauty is, specifically in womanhood.

WHAT DO YOU STRUGGLE WITH AS A WOMAN? AS AN ARTIST?
Being a woman is a struggle because we're supposed to craft and adapt our bodies and mentalities in every single situation. We're also privileged because we're the ones who are by nature able to bear life. In general, we're really empathetic, and our hearts are usually very pure. That's a struggle but also a blessing.

ACKNOWLEDGMENTS

———

I don't know what pushed me into writing a book. I mean, it has always been a dream of mine to write a book, see and read my own words typed on paper, on real book pages. I never thought I could do such a thing while in college, along with all the amazing and harsh experiences I had to face. At first, I was scared to embrace this journey because I didn't have any faith in other people's interest: why would people be interested in knowing about me or my passions? Why should I bother with sharing my own opinions with the general public, such a vast group of people? Are people going to take my ideas or imitate me? What is there to imitate, by the way?

Yes, these might be unnecessary questions. However, while typing this sentence, all I can feel is gratitude, because if there's literally one or two eyes landing on these letters I'm carefully pressing on the laptop's keyboard, it is a blessing. I thank you and your body, both present in this moment. You have taken and still are taking some of your precious time in reading this gem of mine. Thank you.

Your getting to this point of the book makes me feel so honored and grateful. I'm motivated to go forward by enjoying the present moment, which is now filled with new upcoming projects and dreams. Everything that I do is moved by love and passion. If I have made time to bring these words to you, dear reader, it means that I thought of you as someone who deserves a special place in my heart. I was present in doing something that I love, thinking about you. You can either look up or distance yourself from me, but at least, this is the offer I've made. I was present for you. I love doing that.

Thank you, Professor Koester, for this opportunity. I've grown so much while writing this book, and I can't wait to blossom even more. Thank you mamae e babbo, vi amo tanto com todo o meu coração. Thank you Victoria, Alyssa, Antreise, Gianluca, Kenny, Tamara, Mia, Jeffrey, Edoardo, Pietro, Lucilla, Jourden, Andrea, Brian, Ben, Benedetto, Sue, Jiao, Camilla, Chelsea, Felicity, Francesca, Hugo, Jessica, Joël, Jon, Kim, Lex, Lia, Manuela, Mariah, Matilde, Rachel, Rosaria, Sophia, Stefania, Veronica, Michael A., Shawn, Nesta, and Sky.

A huge thanks to New Degree Press and my team of editors, particularly to Cortni, Bailee, Leila, Amanda, and Brian. Wow, now I even know what it is like to write a book: fun and intense. What a journey!

I appreciate and love those who have been present for me. A real present. I love receiving this energy, not going to lie. Thank you, thank you, thank you.

Again, thank you.
Beijos,
Giulia
the curly flower

APPENDIX

INTRODUCTION

"Signs." Aubrey Drake Graham (Drake), Spotify, single written by Young Thug, Supa Dups, Ashante Reid, 40 and Drake, Cash Money and Young Money labels, 2017.

CHAPTER 1

Christie, Shelby. Twitter Post. June 20, 2020, 2:50 PM. https://twitter.com/bronze_bombSHEL/status/1274414224735981569.

Christie, Shelby. Twitter Post. June 29, 2020, 9:53 AM. https://twitter.com/bronze_bombSHEL/status/1277601097885134850?s=20.

CHAPTER 2

Cline, Elizabeth. *The Conscious Closet: The Revolutionary Guide to Looking Good While Doing Good.* New York City: Plume, 2019.

"Facts and Figures about Materials, Waste and Recycling." *United States Environmental Protection Agency (EPA).*

https://www.epa.gov/facts-and-figures-about-materials-waste-and-recycling/national-overview-facts-and-figures-materials.

CHAPTER 3

Duffin, Erin. "The most spoken languages worldwide in 2019." *Statista*. April 3, 2020. https://www.google.com/url?q=https://www.statista.com/statistics/266808/the-most-spoken-languagesworldwide/&sa=D&ust=1594247510446000&usg=AF-QjCNHnvUG9ZrmlLhd1baCi4RaIg1hZoA.

Faez, Farahnaz. "English Education in Italy: Perceptions of Teachers and Professors of English." *Semantic Scholar*. 2011. https://pdfs.semanticscholar.org/8b4a/fecf794a82ac9fbda027e-456910c175a2eac.pdf.

Lyiscott, Jamila. "3 Ways to Speak English." Filmed February 2014 in New York, NY. TED video. https://www.ted.com/talks/jamila_lyiscott_3_ways_to_speak_english.

CHAPTER 4

Gold, Hannah. "Workers Making Fashion Nova Clothing Are Wildly Underpaid." *The Cut*. December 16, 2019. https://www.thecut.com/2019/12/workers-making-fashion-nova-clothing-are-wildly-underpaid.html.

Lin, Grace. "Are You Spending More Than the Average American on 25 Everyday Items?" *GOBankingRates*. April 7, 2020. https://www.gobankingrates.com/saving-money/budgeting/how-much-average-american-spends-daily/?utm_campaign-=944416&utm_source=yahoo.com&utm_content=11.

Moulds, Josephine. "Child labour in the fashion supply chain: Where, why and what can be done." *The Guardian*. https://labs.theguardian.com/unicef-child-labour/.

TEDx Talks. "Life in the Slow Lane: Sustainable Fashion 101 | Tamara Jones | TEDxRyersonU." *YouTube* video, 13:55. June 22, 2017. https://www.youtube.com/watch?v=VwGLPMTYPZY.

The Vision. "Nel mondo vengono acquistate più di 1 mln di bottiglie di plastica al minuto." *Instagram*, February 19, 2020. https://www.instagram.com/p/B8vtxkqofUz/?igshid=1no72i5khdrnw.

CHAPTER 5

Adichie, Chimamanda Ngozi. "The danger of a single story." Filmed July 2009 in Oxford, UK. TED video. https://www.ted.com/talks/chimamanda_ngozi_adichie_the_danger_of_a_single_story?language=en.

Giuffrida, Angela. "More than half of Italians in poll say racist acts are justifiable." *The Guardian*. November 12, 2019. https://www.theguardian.com/world/2019/nov/12/more-than-half-of-italians-in-poll-say-racism-is-justifiable.

Hanh, Thich Nhat. *You Are Here: Discovering the Magic of the Present Moment.* Boulder: Shambhala, 2004.

CONCLUSION

"Growing Up (Sloane's song)," featuring Ed Sheeran, track 5 on *This Unruly Mess I've Made,* Macklemore LLC, 2016.

Made in the USA
Columbia, SC
05 October 2020

22039668R00115